Intellectual Property and Assessing Its Financial Value

CHANDOS
INFORMATION PROFESSIONAL SERIES

Series Editor: Ruth Rikowski
(Email: Rikowskigr@aol.com)

Chandos' new series of books is aimed at the busy information professional. They have been specially commissioned to provide the reader with an authoritative view of current thinking. They are designed to provide easy-to-read and (most importantly) practical coverage of topics that are of interest to librarians and other information professionals. If you would like a full listing of current and forthcoming titles, please visit www.chandospublishing.com.

New authors: we are always pleased to receive ideas for new titles; if you would like to write a book for Chandos, please contact Dr Glyn Jones on g.jones.2@elsevier.com or telephone +44 (0) 1865 843000.

Intellectual Property and Assessing Its Financial Value

With a focus on life sciences

BENEDIKT SAS, PHILIPPE JACOBS,
AND
STANISLAS DE VOCHT

ELSEVIER

AMSTERDAM BOSTON CAMBRIDGE HEIDELBERG LONDON
NEW YORK OXFORD PARIS SAN DIEGO
SAN FRANCISCO SINGAPORE SYDNEY TOKYO
Chandos Publishing is an imprint of Elsevier

CP
CHANDOS
PUBLISHING

Chandos Publishing
Elsevier Limited
The Boulevard
Langford Lane
Kidlington
OX5 1GB
UK
store.elsevier.com/Chandos-Publishing-/IMP_207/

Chandos Publishing is an imprint of Elsevier Limited

Tel: +44 (0) 1865 843000
Fax: +44 (0) 1865 843010
store.elsevier.com

First published in 2014

ISBN: 978-1-84334-792-7 (print)
ISBN: 978-1-78063-475-3 (online)

Chandos Information Professional Series

Library of Congress Control Number: 2014956637

British Library Cataloguing-in-Publication Data.
A catalogue record for this book is available from the British Library.

Typeset in the UK by Concerto.

Contents

List of figures and tables

Figures

Tables

About the authors

Professor Dr Benedikt Sas, senior business developer (IOF), has worked at Ghent University since May 2008 and is currently acting as chief business officer for Food2Know and a professor in the field of corporate and innovation management.

Benedikt obtained his PhD at Ghent University and completed several management courses at Vlerick (Ghent University) and Templeton (University of Oxford). In 1996 he started working as an R&D manager in chemistry for Kemin Europa NV, an international company active in the feed and petfood additive business. Later he became director of the R&D Department and R&D worldwide coordinator for the Kemin Industries Group, covering all life science divisions. In 2001 he was appointed president of a new start-up company, Kemin Pharma.

Benedikt has a significant track record of bringing new products and technologies to market, and closing strategic alliances or licensing deals. He also provides training to PhD and post-doctoral students on business development, licensing, and spin-offs. He is still involved in industry as a member of the board of advisors of several companies, as a consultant, and as a (co)founder and shareholder of new companies. He also provides expertise to working groups of the EU Commission and for courts in Belgium. He is inventor on numerous approved and commercialized patents and the author of peer-reviewed papers.

Dr Philippe Jacobs has been the in-house European patent attorney of UGent TechTransfer since May 2010. In addition, he lectures at the University of Antwerp. Prior to joining UGent he was a director with the IP firm De Clercq & Partners, and a patent attorney in the tech-transfer team of the Flanders Institute for Biotechnology; before this he was a patent counsel in the intellectual property department of Innogenetics, a Belgian biotech company active in healthcare. In addition, Philippe has four years' teaching experience in Rwanda. He holds a PhD in immunology and a master's of science in biological control, both from McGill University, Canada, a diploma in tropical medical biology from the Institute for Tropical Medicine of Antwerp, and a licentiate degree in botany from UGent.

Stanislas De Vocht obtained a master's in law at Ghent University in 2005 and began his career as a lawyer at Ghent Bar, where he combined his internship with a ManaMa in intellectual property rights. In 2007 he started as an in-house legal counsel at UGent TechTransfer, where he was responsible for negotiating agreements and advising internal clients on issues concerning protection and valorization of intellectual property in general. In 2011 he became a self-employed intellectual property consultant, providing services to SMEs and freelancers (such as photographers, writers, and musicians) with regard to their intellectual property and other legal issues. He combined this with a function as professional support lawyer in the IP/IT department of Allen & Overy LLP in Brussels, where he monitored legal developments in the area of intellectual property and communicated these to lawyers and clients.

In May 2013 Stanislas became the IP and technology transfer manager at iMinds, a Flemish research organization involved in ICT.

For general information or technical support please contact:

Prof. Dr Benedikt Sas
Coupure links 653
B-9000 Ghent
T +32 9 264 99 40 F +32 9 264 99 41
Benedikt.Sas@UGent.be

List of acronyms

ACPA	Anticybersquatting Consumer Protection Act (US)
ACTA	Anti-Counterfeiting Trade Agreement
AGP	antibiotic growth promoter
AIA	America Invents Act
BOIP	Benelux Office for Intellectual Property
CAGR	compound annual growth rate
CDA	confidential disclosure agreement
CE	certainty equivalent
COGS	cost of goods sold
CPVO	EU Community Plant Variety Office
CPVR	Community plant variety rights
CTV	constant terminal value
DCF	discounted cash flow
DTA	decision tree analysis
EBIT	earnings before interest and taxes
EBITDA	earnings before interest, taxes, depreciation, and amortization
EPC	European Patent Convention
EPO	European Patent Office
EU	European Union
FRAND	fair, reasonable, and non-discriminatory
FTO	freedom to operate

GATT	General Agreement on Tariffs and Trade
gTLD	generic top-level domain
ICANN	Internet Corporation for Assigned Names and Numbers
IDF	invention disclosure form
IRR	internal rate of return
MTA	material transfer agreement
NDA	non-disclosure agreement
NPV	net present value
OECD	Organisation for Economic Co-operation and Development
OHIM	Office for Harmonization of the Internal Market (EU)
OTC	over the counter
PCT	Patent Cooperation Treaty
PDO	protected designation of origin
PGI	protected geographical indication
PGS	protected geographical status
PIP	principal investigator's plan
PV	present value
R&D	research and development
RADR	risk-adjusted discount rate
RCD	registered Community design (EU)
ROE	return on equity
ROI	return on investment
SEC	Securities and Exchange Commission (US)
SLD	second-level domain
SOP	standard operating procedure
SPC	supplementary protection certificate
TLD	top-level domain
TRIPS	Agreement on Trade-Related Aspects of Intellectual Property Rights
TT	technology transfer

TV	terminal value
UCD	unregistered Community design (EU)
UDPS	Uniform Domain Name Dispute Resolution Policy
UPOV	International Union for the Protection of New Varieties of Plants
US	United States
USPTO	US Patent and Trademark Office
VC	venture capitalist
WACC	weighted average cost of capital
WIPO	World Intellectual Property Organization
WTO	World Trade Organization

1

Overview

Abstract: Most people know a few forms of intellectual property (IP), such as patents or copyright, but there are many others. This chapter provides an overview of the different types of IP, illustrated via the history of the scientist Dr L. Baekeland, who turned several of his innovations into commercial successes. In addition, several tools are presented for maintaining confidentiality to safeguard possible new IP.

Key words: intellectual property, definitions, overview, confidentiality, NDA, CDA, MTA.

Introduction

Creativity is the base of innovation and leads to economic value and competitive advantage. This maxim holds true equally in life sciences as for other areas or industries. Such value may come from a new product/technology, edging out competitors in a market, creating a revenue stream in new territories, or increasing market reputation. This book provides an introduction to intellectual property (IP), assessing its financial value and valorization as applied to life-sciences-related industries, such as biotechnology, food, feed, medicine, and pharmacy. This area of law provides the legal framework for bridging creativity and the value that may come from it. Through the proper use of IP, one has a significantly better chance of converting creativity into economic value.

Intellectual property law recognizes a creator's rights in ideas, creations, innovations, and goodwill. Being intangible, IP differs from real property (land) or personal property (your possessions) that is secured, controlled, and protected using physical means such as fences, alarms, and security staff. Because intellectual property is a product of the mind, there is often no easy way to build a "fence" around it. Protecting IP is very subtle.

Many scientists are good at doing science, but in some (unfortunately rare) cases they also have a good business sense. A nice example is Leo Baekeland (Figure 1.1).

Leo Hendrik Baekeland was born in Sint-Martens-Latem, Belgium, on 14 November 1863. He obtained a PhD in chemistry at Ghent University in 1884, then raised significant funds from various investors and started a company in 1893. The logo of his company, Nepera Chemical, is based on the von Liebig type of kali equipment, often used in chemistry labs (Figure 1.2). Baekeland had a broad range of interests in the use of chemistry for various applications, and in 1893 filed a first patent on the use of fluoride containing salts for the preservation of meat and fish (Figure 1.3).

He also worked on improving the production and quality of photographic paper. His improved paper with the brand name "Velox" could be developed using artificial light, which was a significant advantage over the old photographic paper that needed to be developed using sunlight, which of course depended on the weather conditions (Figure 1.4).

Figure 1.1 Leo Baekeland (1863–1944)

Source: Science Museum, Ghent University.

Figure 1.2 The logo of Baekeland's first company on a package of Velox paper

Source: Science Museum, Ghent University.

Figure 1.3 Baekeland's family on Velox photographic paper

Figure 1.4 Baekeland's patent regarding an antiseptic compound, 4 July 1893

UNITED STATES PATENT OFFICE.

LEO H. BAEKELAND, OF NEW YORK, N. Y.

ANTISEPTIC COMPOUND.

SPECIFICATION forming part of Letters Patent No. 500,549, dated July 4, 1893.

Application filed June 27, 1892. Serial No. 438,193. (No specimens.)

To all whom it may concern:

Be it known that I, LEO H. BAEKELAND, a citizen of the Kingdom of Belgium, and a resident of the city, county, and State of New York, have invented certain new and useful Improvements in Compounds for Preserving Meat and Fish, of which the following is a specification.

In studying the antiseptic action of fluorid of sodium and fluorid of potassium on meat, fish and other perishable products, I discovered that these antiseptic properties of fluorid salts were specially useful for practical purposes when mixed with common salt or chlorid of sodium. In making a series of ... ing the action of the fluorids on the digestive fluids. These experiments established the important fact, that these fluorids exert no injurious effects on the digestive fluids like other antiseptic substances and they differ thereby from the other antiseptic substances heretofore used. It was further discovered that the fluorids under certain circumstances increase the digestive action of ptyalin, pepsin and trypsin and that this beneficial action was further developed in the presence of a sufficient quantity of chlorid of sodium. The admixture of chlorid of sodium with the fluorids constitutes thereby a decided improvement in the manufacture of antiseptic substances:

Baekeland sold his company in 1899 to Eastman Kodak for US$750,000 and, inspired by Benjamin Franklin, moved to the United States. He reinvested his money, bought a large estate in Yonkers, New York, and formed a research team of 40 chemists to study the chemical reaction of phenols and formaldehyde (Figure 1.5).

On 7 December 1909 his famous patent was issued for the production of the first true "plastic" ever (Figure 1.6), which was later given the brand name "Bakelite" (Figure 1.7).

Baekeland subsequently filed several other patents on the use of Bakelite®, such as the production of "sound records" using Bakelite (patent dated 30 December 1913, Figure 1.8). He also designed a lot of lab equipment using Bakelite for his friends at Ghent University.

In 1910 Baekeland established the General Bakelite Company, which in 1939 was sold to and merged with the Union Carbide Carbon Corporation to form the Union Carbide Plastics Company. For this transaction, Baekeland received US$51.5 million. By the time he died in 1944 the production of Bakelite and/or analogues had reached 175,000 tons, which was used by over 35 other large companies to produce more than 15,000 different objects in Bakelite material (Figure 1.9).

Figure 1.5 Baekeland in his lab

Figure 1.6 The famous Bakelite patent, dated 7 December 1909

UNITED STATES PATENT OFFICE.

LEO H. BAEKELAND, OF YONKERS, NEW YORK.

CONDENSATION PRODUCT OF PHENOL AND FORMALDEHYDE AND METHOD OF MAKING THE SAME.

942,700. Specification of Letters Patent. Patented Dec. 7, 1909.

No Drawing. Application filed December 4, 1907. Serial No. 405,021.

To all whom it may concern:

Be it known that I, LEO H. BAEKELAND, a citizen of the United States, residing at Yonkers, in the county of Westchester and State of New York, have invented certain new and useful Improvements in Condensation Products of Phenols and Formaldehyde and Methods of Making the Same, of which the following is a specification.

character and contains the initial products of chemical condensation. The liquids are readily separated, and the aqueous solution may be rejected, or the water may be eliminated by evaporation. The oily or viscous liquid obtained as above described, and hereinafter referred to as the "initial condensation product," is found to be soluble in or miscible with alcohol, acetone, phenol, and

Figure 1.7 The trademark for Bakelite

Figure 1.8 Patent dated 30 December 1913 on the use of Bakelite for the production of sound records, and photo of a record with the voice of Baekeland

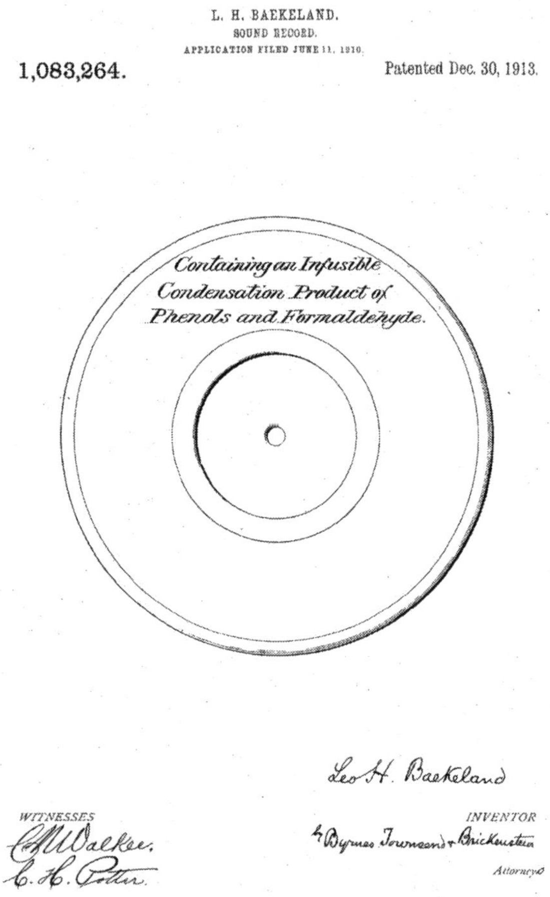

Source: Science Museum, Ghent University.

Figure 1.9 A radio case and scientific instruments made out of Bakelite

Source: Science Museum, Ghent University.

In this story of Baekeland, we come across several types of IP.

- *Patent*. Patents may be granted for the invention of any new, economically relevant, and useful product, process, or machine, or any new, useful improvement thereof. A patent is a property right that grants the inventor or owner the right to exclude others from producing, using, selling, or advertising the invention as defined by the patent's claims in a specific country or territory for a period of 20 years.
- *Trade secret*. Generally, a trade secret is any formula, manufacturing process, method of business, technical know-how, etc. that gives its

holder a competitive advantage and is secret. The legal definition of a trade secret and the protection afforded to its owner vary from country to country, and generally the owner needs to demonstrate established protocols to maintain secrecy. The most famous examples are the ingredients and production of Coca-Cola®.

- *Trademark*. A trademark is a word, phrase, design, or combination thereof which identifies and distinguishes the source of the products or services of one party in comparison to others – Coca-Cola is again an example. Trademarks can build brands, corporate identity, and competitive advantage. Domain names for websites are related to trademarks.
- *Copyright*. Copyrights protect original works of authorship fixed in a tangible, reproducible form. Copyrighted works include literary, dramatic, and musical compositions, movies, photos, artwork, computer programs, cooking recipes, etc. Copyright protects the expression of an idea, but not the idea itself. Software and databases are specific cases related to copyright.
- *Designs and models*. These are protected in the United States as design patents and in the European Union as registered Community designs.

Depending on the industry, there are sometimes additional types of IP rights available.

- *Recognition of traditional foods*. To improve recognition of traditional food products relating to a specific region, the European Union has created protected geographical status (PGS), which has three types of label – protected designation of origin (PDO), protected geographical indication (PGI), and traditional specialty guaranteed.
- *Breeders' rights*. In agriculture there are specific rights for people who generate new plant varieties. Also known as plant variety rights in the European Union, these are rights granted to the breeder of a new variety of plant that give her/him exclusive control over the propagating material (including seed, tissue culture, etc.) and harvested material (cut flowers, fruit, foliage) of the new variety for a number of years. In the United States these are plant patents, and in the European Union plant varieties are protected by Community plant variety rights (CPVRs) issued by the Community Plant Variety Office (CPVO, discussed below).
- *Supplementary protection certificate*. In some life-science-related cases it is possible to extend the lifetime of a patent. In Europe a

supplementary protection certificate (SPC) is a *sui generis* extension of a patent under a specific, different, set of rights. This type of right is available for medicinal products, such as drugs, and plant protection products, such as insecticides and herbicides.

Some intellectual property rights are granted after a registration procedure and come with a "certificate" (Figure 1.10). Other types of IP do not require registration, do not come with a certificate, and are covered by law (Figure 1.11). There are some differences between countries related to registered or non-registered IP (discussed below).

As noted, in our example of Leo Baekeland we came across several types of IP: trademarks (the name Nepera Chemical® and its logo, Bakelite®, and Velox®), patents (e.g. on the antiseptic compound, on Bakelite, and on uses of Bakelite), trade secrets (Baekeland's work to improve photographic paper), and designs (e.g. the radio case shown in Figure 1.9).

There are a variety of pitfalls that pop up and need to be tackled. Different rules apply to different types of IP. Accordingly, you may forfeit your rights if you do not take the appropriate measures to secure and protect them. Thus it is important to understand the types of IP protection and the respective rules that govern each type of IP.

It is crucial to think first about possible new IP and its protection before actually publishing or sharing information with third parties (Figure 1.12). This is very important! Doing it the other way around, all IP rights will/can be lost. Trade secrets of course can never be published and need to be kept secret.

It is also important before you begin researching or developing a new idea to see what already exists in the literature, but more important to investigate the existence of IP on this subject. If a lot of relevant IP exists, all your efforts may be worthless and therefore abandoning the idea or project could be the better option.

It is important to understand that IP rights are negative. They are used to stop competitors from using your creation. There is no need to obtain an IP right to start commercializing. However, if you want to be able to stop competitors entering your market, having (a bundle of) IP rights will help.

Once secured, a company can enforce its IP rights against a competitor. A notable example is the court case of *Kemin Foods v. Pigmentos*.[1] Kemin Foods filed a suit against Pigmentos for infringement of two patents directed to purified lutein that is extracted from plants such as marigolds (*Tagetes erecta*). Currently, lutein is sold under the trade name

Figure 1.10 IP with a certificate

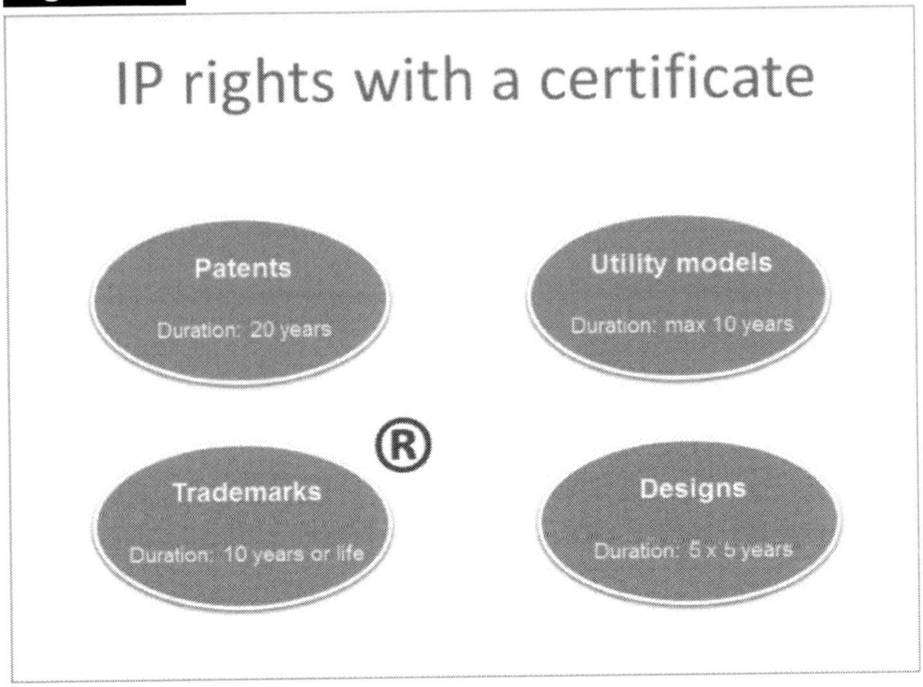

Figure 1.11 IP without a certificate

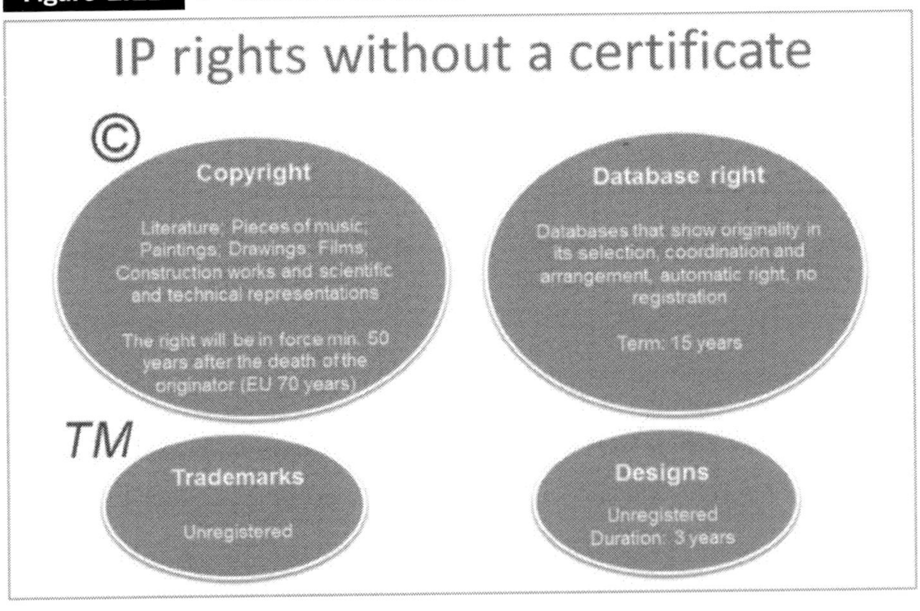

Figure 1.12 First protect IP, then publish

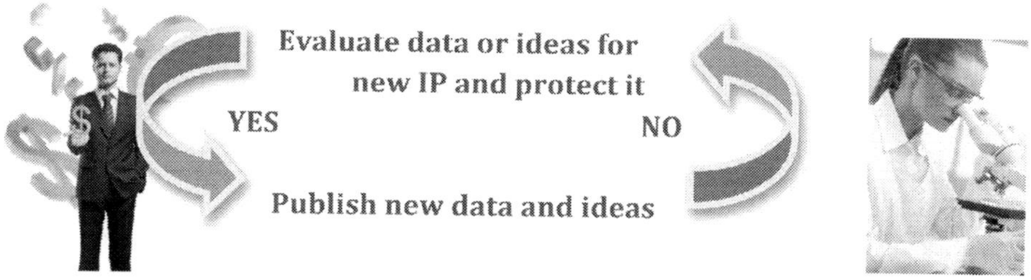

FloraGlo® as a nutriceutical for the prevention of age-related macular degradation. The defendant filed a counterclaim seeking a declaratory judgment that Kemin's patents were invalid and unenforceable. The court of appeals affirmed the district court's holding that the patent claims were valid, and that Kemin Foods was entitled to damages based on the defendant's infringement of its patents.

Tools for maintaining confidentiality and safeguarding IP

Confidential disclosure agreements (CDAs), which are also called non-disclosure agreements (NDAs) or secrecy agreements, refer to a contract that protects confidential or trade secret information ("confidential information") from disclosure to third parties. NDAs are commonly included as a part of an employment contract, and also included in, or form, a separate agreement with licensees, vendors, contractors, and sometimes customers.

A CDA should include the following provisions.

- A clear definition of the information that is to be held in confidence.
- Instructions on how the information should be marked or identified, for example with a "Confidential" stamp or label.
- A specific recitation of the limited purposes for which the confidential information can be used.
- A recitation that the receiving party cannot breach the confidential relationship, induce others to breach it, or induce others to acquire the confidential information by improper means; and a list of exceptions to the confidentiality requirements.

- The time period over which the information must be held in confidence. Five or eight years are most common.
- A provision defining the remedy available to the non-breaching party in the event of a breach or impending breach, e.g. clauses on arbitration.
- Jurisdiction and governing laws.
- Signature date.
- Signatures of legal representatives (it is crucial that the CDA is signed by legal representatives in order to be binding).

CDAs can be one way (one party providing confidential information to another) or mutual (both parties exchanging confidential information).

When, next to information, materials are exchanged, it is more advisable to sign a material transfer agreement (MTA), which contains articles on the nature of the materials which are given to a third party and on what this party is allowed to do and/or cannot do with these materials.

Although damages may be available against the discloser, an actual public disclosure cannot be undone. This could result in inadvertent loss of the ability to seek patent protection in many countries that have absolute novelty requirements. While the United States allows a one-year grace period from the date of first public use or disclosure of an invention, if the owner of the confidential information is unaware of the disclosure, US patent rights could also be lost. Furthermore, any trade secret information that is publicly disclosed is no longer a trade secret.

Examples of a CDA and an MTA are presented in Appendixes 1 and 2.

Awareness building

Awareness building around IP is one of the cornerstones of a successful IP program. Inadvertent disclosure of confidential information or new inventions that are being developed can easily result in any potential intellectual property rights being lost or, worse, landing directly in a competitor's hands. The only way to address this effectively is to train employees such that they understand the ramifications of their actions and the potential cost to the company in terms of lost IP rights and lost profits on new products or developments that cannot be protected.

Accurate record keeping

Patents

Especially under the first-to-invent system in the United States (valid until 2013), it is important for inventors to document when they first conceived an invention, as well as all the activities that were carried out in actually "reducing the invention to practice", either by making or carrying out the invention or by filing a patent application for it, referred to as "constructive" reduction to practice.

All work and research activities should be documented in written form, and should be dated and witnessed by another person. A preferred form for documenting this type of information is an inventor's notebook, which is a bound book with numbered pages where details can be recorded. Each page includes a space where it can be dated and witnessed once the information has been entered. Completed notebooks should be kept for reference, since it may be years before the information is actually needed. Different systems exist that can help in registering when an idea was first conceived (several of these systems are explained in Chapter 5).

As mentioned, in the United States a first-to-invent system for patents was followed until 2013, whereas in Europe patents are granted on a first-to-file basis. It is clear that for IP-related possibilities and legislation, differences can exist between countries, although many are working towards harmonization.

The US system is moving towards the European one. On 16 September 2011 President Obama signed the America Invents Act (AIA), which contains sweeping changes to the US patent system: changes regarding the US Patent and Trademark Office (USPTO) moving towards the European first to file, fees (15 percent increase), the substantive patent law, and new post-ground-review proceedings. Except for the fee changes, most provisions went into effect in 2013.

From 2013 onwards the United States moved to a first-to-file system, similar to the European situation. Nevertheless, there is a snag, since the United States stipulates that it must be "the first inventor" who needs to file. Hence if you can demonstrate and prove that you are the first inventor, but someone stole your invention and filed a patent application before you, the patent will most probably be awarded to you as the first inventor filing an application.

Another document that a company, university, or institute should have is an invention submission form, also called an invention disclosure form

(IDF). This should include sections for a complete description of the invention, as well as any potentially critical events that occur, such as a disclosure to others. This form serves several purposes.

- It can serve as the vehicle for in-house review and a determination of whether patent protection is going to be pursued.
- If the company, university, or institute proceeds with a patent application, it can act as the vehicle for transmitting information on the invention to patent counsel for searching and/or the preparation of a patent application.
- It documents and helps to prove that a person, company, or university is working on a new idea or invention.

An IDF example is presented in Appendix 3.

Trade secrets

Trade secret protection depends on defining and following a strict set of policies for handling information that is being protected as a trade secret. Trade secret policies should be documented in a policy manual or standard operating procedure (SOP), and all employees who have access to the trade secret information should receive training on handling it and be required periodically to review the company's policy regarding treatment of such information.

Policies should include how to identify and mark trade secrets, including information or technology under development. Identification can be as broad as "all information related to project x" or as detailed as a specific formula for a product, such as an ingredient for a recipe or mix, and can be set by management or an advisory board. Marking should be on both physical and electronic documents, using labels such as "Confidential", "Secret", "Trade Secret", "Classified", or "Proprietary Information" of the company, organization, or university. Different labels indicating the level of secrecy can also be initiated, describing who can have access to what level.

Access to the trade secret information should be on a need-to-know basis inside the organization. Access should also be on a "log in, log out" basis, whether on paper or electronically. Any electronically stored or transmitted information should be encrypted based on a defined procedure.

A policy should also define storage of the information when an employee is away from his/her work station, and may include a locked or secured central storage area. The reason for this high level of security is that in a misappropriation lawsuit a court's inquiry will not only focus on the bad acts of the accused party, but will also examine and consider whether the company defending its trade secret rights adequately maintained and safeguarded its secrets.

Notes

1. *Kemin Foods, LC versus Pigmentos Vegetales Del Centro SA de CV*, 464 F.3d 1339, Fed. Cir., 2006.

2

Patents

Abstract: This chapter zooms in on patents as important intellectual property rights. It describes what a patent is and why the patent system exists. Differences between the United States and Europe with regard to what types of patents – such as US utility, plant, and design patents – exist are highlighted and exemplified. The chapter further elaborates on inventorship, ownership, and possible pathways to obtain a patent. A clear description of what content should be part of a patent application and how claims – which define the scope of protection – are constructed is also given. The chapter covers what is and is not patentable, how costly patents usually are, and what is meant by continuing applications. Finally, some information about laws and treaties that govern the patent system and the existence of supplementary protection certificates is provided.

Key words: patent, invention, patentability, (patent) law.

What is a patent?

A patent is a set of exclusive rights (a right to exclude others) granted by a country(s) to a patent owner (an inventor(s) or his/her assignee) for a limited period of time after submission and rigorous evaluation of a patentable invention of economic importance, to prevent others exploiting the invention described in the patent.

The word *patent* originates from the Latin *patere*, which means "to lay open" (i.e. to make available for public inspection). The term *patent*, *brevet* (French), or *octrooi* (Dutch), which originally denoted a royal decree, means "open for public reading" or "granting exclusive rights to a person".

In 1473 Venice issued a law containing some of the basic principles of a patent. The law stated that it needed to be an object, not an idea, it should be registered at the administrative office, and the fully developed object needed to be novel and inventive, ready for use, and never have been made before in the territory. The period of protection was ten years.

With the expansion of trade, the patent concept of Venice spread throughout Europe. Patent protection was of great importance to the American rebels in 1776 – George Washington himself was an inventor. Since it was of such importance, patents were included in the US Constitution under Article 1, section 8. Congress later released the Patent Act in 1790.

The first US patent (Figure 2.1) was awarded to Samuel Hopkins of Pennsylvania on 31 July 1790 for an improvement in the making of potash and pearl ash by a new apparatus and process. This first patent was also signed by Washington.

Globalization of the patent system started in the nineteenth century. This resulted in the Unions Treaty of Paris of 1883, the Patent

Figure 2.1 The first US patent (X1), awarded to S. Hopkins in 1790

Cooperation Treaty (PCT) of 1970, and the Trade Related Aspects of Intellectual Property Rights (TRIPS) treaty of the World Trade Organization (WTO) of 1994.

The need for uniform regulation is growing. In mid-2000 the member states of the World Intellectual Property Organization (WIPO) signed the Patent Law Treaty. Currently, negotiations are ongoing about the Substantive Patent Law Treaty: discussions started in 2000, and the latest (fifteenth) session was held in October 2010. More recently, 25 EU member states (but not Spain and Italy) have embarked on enhanced cooperation with a view to creating unitary patent protection for their territories. In practice this means you can indicate that a patent granted by the European Patent Office (EPO) applies for these 25 states. This new measure may come into effect in mid-2015. And the USPTO recently (March 2013) harmonized its patent law with most other jurisdictions by introducing, among other changes, the "first-to-invent" principle.

The number of patents filed by a company, person, or country is often used, according to the Organisation for Economic Co-operation and Development (OECD, 2010), as one measure of the degree and/or performance of innovation (Figure 2.2).

A patent gives you *the right to exclude others* from making, using, selling, offering for sale, or importing the patented invention, and

Figure 2.2 Triadic patent families per capita (2005–2007)

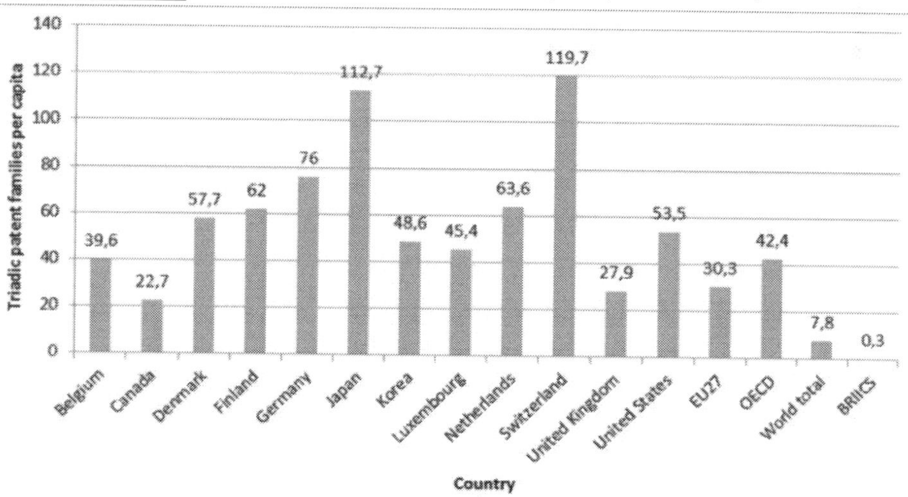

Source: OECD data.

Note: A triadic patent is a patent which is protected in the three major markets: the United States, Europe, and Japan.

creates barriers for competitors to enter the market. Such barriers often facilitate licensing arrangements where some of the patent rights can be transferred or access can be given to other parties. For example, a company can grant a license to one company to produce a patented invention, while granting a second license to another company to use or sell the invention. Developing a strong portfolio of patent rights (i.e. barriers to entry) can be attractive to investors and can create new business opportunities by reducing the risks of competition. A patent is an asset of (normally) significant value.

Some other types of IP rights are referred to as patents, depending on the governing law of a specific territory. For example, in the United States industrial design rights are called design patents (they protect the visual design of objects that are not purely utilitarian). In Europe designs are not protected under patent regulation, but under EU Community designs. Plant breeders' rights are sometimes, as in the United States, called plant patents. In Europe plant varieties are protected by so-called plant variety rights and not by patents.

A utility model is a statutory monopoly granted for a limited time in exchange for an inventor providing sufficient teaching of his or her invention to permit a person of ordinary skill in the relevant art to perform the invention. The rights conferred by utility models laws are similar to those granted by patent laws, but are more suited to what may be considered "incremental inventions". Terms such as "petty patent", "innovation patent", "minor patent", and "small patent" may also be considered to fall within the definition of "utility model". This right is available in a number of national legislations. It is very similar to the patent, but usually has a shorter term (often 15 years – e.g. Brazil) and less stringent patentability requirements.

On a published patent application or patent (also known as the certificate) you can find much crucial information. After the front page, as displayed in Figure 2.3, the description part follows, explaining the invention and giving examples (what actually was done). The claims can be found at the end of the patent and provide vital details of the technology "claimed", i.e. the claims which determine the scope and boundaries of protection offered by the patent (Figure 2.4).

When a patent is being investigated and not yet approved (known as "status A"), it is called a "patent application". Published patent applications attach at the end of the document a list of possible prior art that the patent examiner at the patent office has identified. It often provides a lot of useful information when studying "freedom to operate" (FTO, discussed further below).

Figure 2.3 Information found on a patent

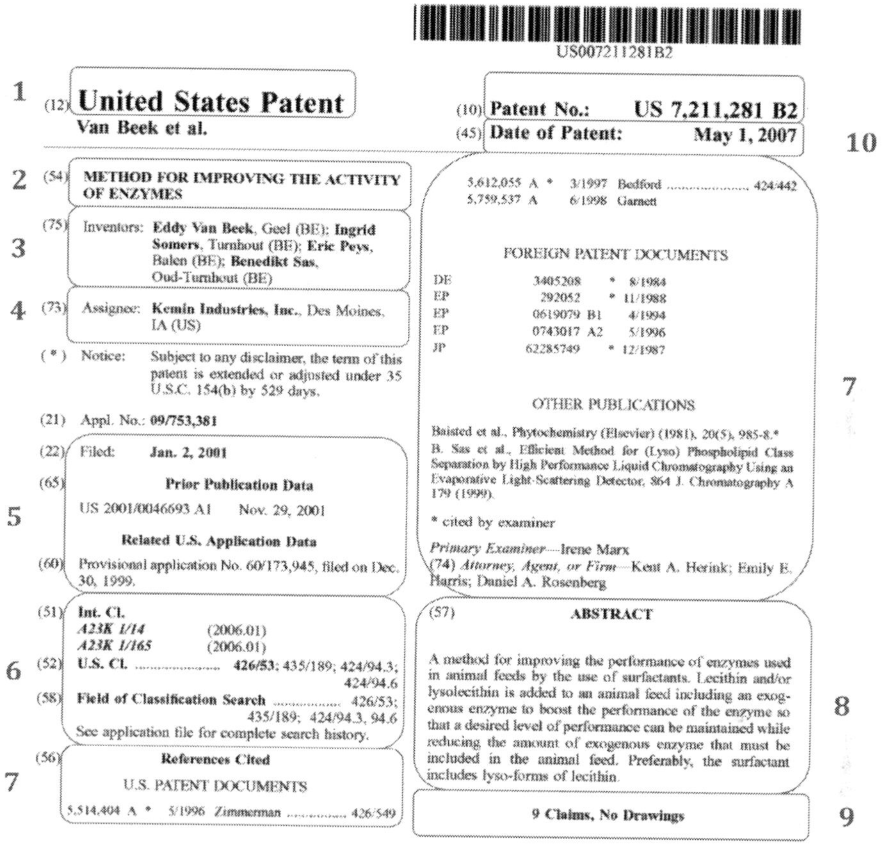

US007211281B2

(12) **United States Patent**
Van Beek et al.

(10) **Patent No.: US 7,211,281 B2**
(45) **Date of Patent: May 1, 2007**

(54) **METHOD FOR IMPROVING THE ACTIVITY OF ENZYMES**

(75) Inventors: **Eddy Van Beek**, Geel (BE); **Ingrid Somers**, Turnhout (BE); **Eric Peys**, Balen (BE); **Benedikt Sas**, Oud-Turnhout (BE)

(73) Assignee: **Kemin Industries, Inc.**, Des Moines, IA (US)

(*) Notice: Subject to any disclaimer, the term of this patent is extended or adjusted under 35 U.S.C. 154(b) by 529 days.

(21) Appl. No.: **09/753,381**

(22) Filed: **Jan. 2, 2001**

(65) **Prior Publication Data**

US 2001/0046693 A1 Nov. 29, 2001

Related U.S. Application Data

(60) Provisional application No. 60/173,945, filed on Dec. 30, 1999.

(51) **Int. Cl.**
A23K 1/14 (2006.01)
A23K 1/165 (2006.01)

(52) **U.S. Cl.** **426/53**; 435/189; 424/94.3; 424/94.6

(58) **Field of Classification Search** 426/53; 435/189; 424/94.3, 94.6
See application file for complete search history.

(56) **References Cited**

U.S. PATENT DOCUMENTS

5,514,404 A * 5/1996 Zimmerman 426/549
5,612,055 A * 3/1997 Bedford 424/442
5,759,537 A 6/1998 Garnett

FOREIGN PATENT DOCUMENTS

DE	3405208	*	8/1984
EP	292052	*	11/1988
EP	0619079 B1		4/1994
EP	0743017 A2		5/1996
JP	62285749	*	12/1987

OTHER PUBLICATIONS

Baisted et al., Phytochemistry (Elsevier) (1981), 20(5), 985-8.*
B. Sas et al., Efficient Method for (Lyso) Phospholipid Class Separation by High Performance Liquid Chromatography Using an Evaporative Light-Scattering Detector, 864 J. Chromatography A 179 (1999).

* cited by examiner

Primary Examiner—Irene Marx
(74) *Attorney, Agent, or Firm*—Kent A. Herink; Emily E. Harris; Daniel A. Rosenberg

(57) **ABSTRACT**

A method for improving the performance of enzymes used in animal feeds by the use of surfactants. Lecithin and/or lysolecithin is added to an animal feed including an exogenous enzyme to boost the performance of the enzyme so that a desired level of performance can be maintained while reducing the amount of exogenous enzyme that must be included in the animal feed. Preferably, the surfactant includes lyso-forms of lecithin.

9 Claims, No Drawings

Notes

1. Country and patent number (with status, e.g. A = under examination, B = granted).
2. Title.
3. Name and home address of the inventor(s).
4. Assignee, i.e. who owns the patent.
5. Filing date, priority date, and publication date.
6. Classification.
7. References.
8. Abstract.
9. Claims.
10. Date of patent (after it is examined and granted).

Figure 2.4 **The claims related to the patent presented in Figure 2.3**

The invention claimed is:

1. A method for improving the degradation of the neutral detergent fiber in an animal feed with a combination of exogenous enzymes, comprising the step of adding an effective amunt of a surfactant to an animal feed containing a combination of exogenous enzymes comprising xylanase, α-amylase, α-galactosidase, β-glucanase cellulase, lipase, and protease, wherein the surfactant is a lecithins composition enzymatically enriched in lysophospholipids to contain at least about 5% by weight of lysophospholipids to the amount of lysophospholipids plus phospholipids, to degrade the neutral detergent fiber in the animal feed.

US 7,211,281 B2

2. The method as defined in claim 1, wherein said animal feed includes from between about 10 weight percent to about 55 weight percent of a small cereal grain.

3. The method as defined in claim 2, wherein said small cereal grain is selected from the group consisting of wheat and barley.

4. The method as defined in claim 3, wherein said enzyme is added to said animal feed in an amount to provide exogenous xylanase activity of between about 100 and about 50 000 units per kilogram of said animal feed.

5. The method as defined in claim 4, wherein said surfactant is included in an amount that is between about 0.025 and about 0.200 grams/kilogram of the animal feed.

6. The method as defined in claim 1, wherein said surfactant is included in an amount that comprises between about 0.025 and about 0.200 grams/kilogram of the animal feed.

7. The method as defined in claim 1, wherein the degradation of neutral detergent fiber is increased by at least at least about 50% over neutral detergent fiber degradation by the combination of exogenous enzyme without the surfactant.

8. The method as defined in claim 1, wherein the protease is added in an amount between about 0.1% and about 1% by weight of the other exogenous enzymes and surfactant.

9. A method of reducing the amount of exogenous enzyme required to achieve a preselected level of degradation of neutral detergent fiber in an animal feed, comprising the step of adding an effective amount of a surfactant to an animal feed containing a combination of exogenous enzymes comprising α-amylase, α-galactosidase, β-glucanase cellulase, lipase and xylanase; a protease; wherein the surfactant is a lecithins composition enzymatically enriched in lysophospholipids to contain at least about 5% by weight of lysophospholipids to the amount of lysophospholipids plus phospholipids, and wherein the amount of the exogenous enzyme is reduced by up to about 50% without a reduction in degradation of neutral detergent fiber.

As mentioned, a patent is not a right to practice or use the invention. Rather, it provides the right to exclude others from making, using, selling, offering for sale, or importing the patented invention for the term of the patent, which is usually 20 years from the filing date subject to the payment of maintenance fees (also known as renewal fees). A patent is, in effect, a limited property right that a government offers to inventors in exchange for their agreement to share the details of their inventions with the public. Like any other property right, this asset/patent may be sold, licensed, mortgaged, assigned, transferred, given away, or simply abandoned.

Several types of patents are issued by the USPTO: utility, design, and plant patents. Utility patents are the most common and protect functional innovations, including "any new and useful process, machine, manufacture, or composition of matter, or any new and useful improvement thereof". Utility patents protect the structure or function of an invention for a term of 20 years from their earliest effective filing date. Most other countries (those governed by the EPO, Japan, Korea) also have this (main) type of patent.

Design patents protect "any new, original, and ornamental design for an article of manufacture" for a term of 14 years from their issue date. The subject matter of a design patent may relate to the configuration or shape of an article, to the surface ornamentation on an article, or to both. If a design is primarily the result of an article's function, a utility model (or even a utility patent) may be preferable over a design patent. Not all countries have this type of patent – e.g. Europe, where designs and plant varieties are protected via other means. Clarification of the difference between a utility model and a design patent is best done via an example. In Figure 2.5 a design patent is presented regarding a bottle in the shape of a cow in which milk can be stored. Its function is mainly ornamental. Figure 2.6 shows a new utility model of milk bottle which is rigid and square, allowing more bottles to be stored in cardboard box compared to round bottles.

Hence in the United States there are three categories of patents:

- utility patents
- design patents
- plant patents.

In Europe it is a bit different.

- Utility patents exist, similar to in the United States.

Figure 2.5 Example of a design patent related to a milk bottle

US00D472461S

(12) **United States Design Patent**
Yourist

(10) **Patent No.:** **US D472,461 S**
(45) **Date of Patent:** ** **Apr. 1, 2003**

(54) **BOTTLE WITH COW DESIGN**

(75) Inventor: **Sheldon Yourist**, York, PA (US)

(73) Assignee: **Graham Packaging Company, L.P.**, York, PA (US)

(**) Term: **14 Years**

(21) Appl. No.: **29/158,230**

(22) Filed: **Apr. 2, 2002**

(51) **LOC (7) Cl.** **09-01**
(52) **U.S. Cl.** **D9/318**
(58) **Field of Search** D9/307, 310, 318, D9/500–502, 549, 556, 559; 215/382–384, 400; D21/659, 610

(56) **References Cited**

U.S. PATENT DOCUMENTS

D189,880 S	*	3/1961	Blake	D21/659
D219,853 S	*	2/1971	Swanner	D9/318 X
D240,240 S	*	6/1976	Orenstein	D21/610
D265,973 S	*	8/1982	Gombert	D9/503 X
D367,422 S	*	2/1996	Chuang	D9/310

* cited by examiner

Primary Examiner—Terry A. Wallace
(74) *Attorney, Agent, or Firm*—Venable; James R. Burdett; Keith G. Haddaway

(57) **CLAIM**

The ornamental design for a bottle with cow design, as shown and described.

DESCRIPTION

FIG. **1** is a front perspective view of a bottle with cow design showing my new design;
FIG. **2** is a front elevation view thereof;
FIG. **3** is a rear elevation view thereof;
FIG. **4** is a left side elevation view thereof;
FIG. **5** is a right side elevation view thereof;
FIG. **6** is a top plan view thereof; and,
FIG. **7** is a bottom plan view thereof.
The broken lines are for illustrative purposes only and form no part of the claimed design.

1 Claim, 4 Drawing Sheets

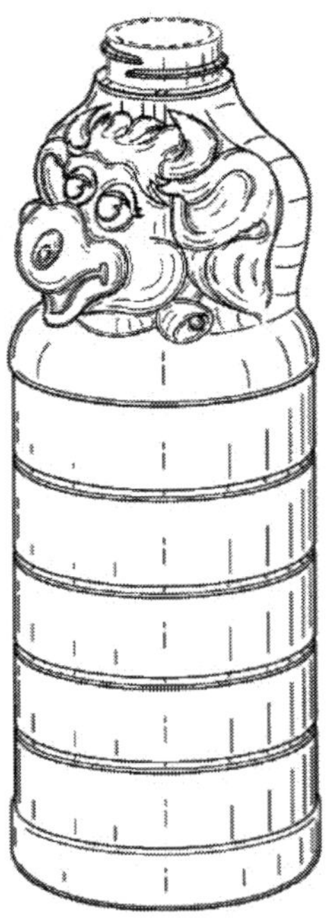

Figure 2.6 Example of a utility patent related to a milk bottle

United States Patent [19] — [11] **4,127,206**

Virog, Jr. et al. — [45] **Nov. 28, 1978**

[54] **MILK BOTTLES**

[75] Inventors: **John J. Virog, Jr.**, Massapequa Park; **Leo Von Hagel**, North Massapequa, both of N.Y.; **Richard L. Platte**, Ann Arbor, Mich.

[73] Assignee: **Honeywell Farms, Inc.**, New York, N.Y.

[21] Appl. No.: **829,966**

[22] Filed: **Sep. 1, 1977**

Related U.S. Application Data

[63] Continuation of Ser. No. 731,294, Oct. 12, 1976, Pat. No. 4,046,275.

[51] **Int. Cl.**[2] **B65D 23/00**

[52] **U.S. Cl.** .... **215/1 C**; 215/100 A

[58] **Field of Search** .... 215/1 C, 100 A, 31

[56] **References Cited**

U.S. PATENT DOCUMENTS

3,434,635	3/1969	Mason	215/1 C
3,443,710	5/1969	Hills	215/100 A
3,708,082	1/1973	Platte	215/1 C
3,784,040	1/1974	Douglas	215/1 C

Primary Examiner—R. E. Hart
Attorney, Agent, or Firm—Abner Sheffer

[57] **ABSTRACT**

A three-quart thin-walled blow molded plastic milk bottle of novel and useful construction.

15 Claims, 8 Drawing Figures

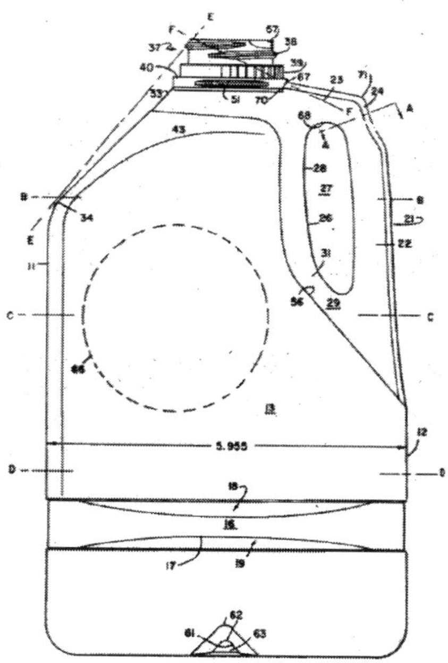

- Designs are not protected as patents, but as EU Community designs.
- Plant varieties are not protected as patents, but breeders' rights are protected under CPVR regulations.

US design patents versus EU Community designs

According to WIPO statistics, the number of design patents is increasing significantly. In 1990 only 1,758 design patents were issued in the United States, versus 14,732 in 1999.

In the United States designs are protected under the patent legislation as patents. Articles 25 and 26 of TRIPS of the WTO cover the protection of industrial designs on a worldwide basis. Deposits can be done via WIPO. National legislation can overrule this, but the European Union and other countries honor it.

Since 1 April 2003 designs are protected in the European Union under the Community design legislation. Registered Community designs (RCDs) can be protected for a maximum of 25 years and unregistered Community designs (UCDs) are protected for a period of three years after first publication. Registrations can be done in a simple way and for a modest cost at the Office for Harmonization of the Internal Market (OHIM).

The application costs for an RCD vary from €230 for a single application to €50 per registration for more than 11 applications. The publication cost varies from €120 for one publication to €30 per registration for more than 11 registrations. The renewal fee after every five years is €90. This is much cheaper (approximately 70 percent) than a design patent in the United States.

A design or model is considered to indicate the appearance as a whole or partially, specifically lines, shape, texture, materials, colors, and decoration. It can be a single item or a complex product composed from various parts, packaging, "get-up" (how something is presented, e.g. the interior), a logo, symbols, etc.

The requirements for an RCD are:

- novelty
- having its own identity/characteristic, i.e. the impression of difference a common user gets in relation to a previous or old model.

Designs and models can be (out-)licensed or sold, but need to be registered and published by the OHIM.

Let us look at an example. Pipettes are small tools that are often used by scientists. Running a search on pipettes and registered Community designs, we find 348 deposits (OHIM, 2014). Some examples are presented in Figure 2.7.

For a UCD no registration is required and no fees need to be paid. Protection is only valid for a period of three years. In some cases this is sufficient, e.g. fashion. The only requirement is that the first publication needs to be done in the European Union and not in any other country beforehand.

US plant patents versus EU plant variety protection

In most countries plants and/or plant parts can be covered by patent claims provided that the applications comply with the necessary standards and requirements in that specific country for patentability. In the United States any living organism, including plants, that is the product of human intervention can be patented. Hence in the United States plant varieties can be patented – often referred to as plant breeders' rights (PBRs). In Europe plant varieties are not patentable, but a genetically modified plant can be patented as long as no genetically modified varieties are specifically claimed. Transgenic plants are thus patentable in Europe if they are not restricted to a specific plant variety but represent a broader plant group; and plant cells are considered as microbiological products and are thus patentable. Countries can on a voluntary base join the International Union for the Protection of New Varieties of Plants

Figure 2.7 Examples of pipette-related registered Community designs

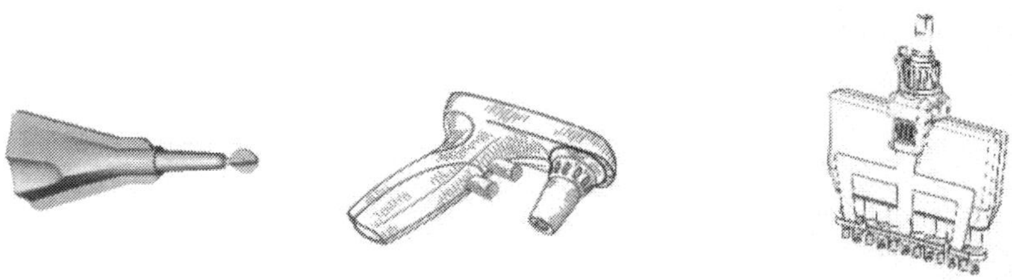

Design #: 000158803-0001 Merial Ltd. (29/3/2004)

Design #: 000203799-0001 Heathrow Scientific LLC. (14/7/2004)

Design #: 001065700-0001 Gilson Sas (5/1/2009)

(UPOV). This convention requires members to provide an intellectual property right (a PBR) for plant varieties.

With PBRs, the breeder can choose to commercialize the variety exclusively, or to license it to others. To qualify for these exclusive PBRs a variety must be new, distinct, uniform, and stable (Table 2.1). A variety is new if it has not been commercialized for more than one year in the country of protection; it is distinct if it differs from all other known varieties by one or more important botanical characteristic, such as height, maturity, color, etc.; it is uniform if the characteristics are consistent from plant to plant within the variety; and it is stable if the plant characteristics are genetically fixed and therefore remain the same from generation to generation, or after a cycle of reproduction in the case of hybrid varieties. The breeder must also give the variety an acceptable "denomination", which becomes its generic name and must be used by anyone who markets the variety.

Typically, plant variety rights are granted by national offices after examination. Seed is submitted to the plant variety office, which grows it for one or more seasons to check that it is distinct, stable, and uniform. If these tests are passed, exclusive rights are granted for a period of 20 years (25 years for trees and vines). Annual renewal fees are required to maintain the rights.

An example is presented in Figure 2.8, where Olesen et al. claimed a new variety of rose called "Poulmona" (US20040025209 P1 dated 5 February 2004).

In Europe, plant varieties as such cannot be patented. Plant varieties and essentially biological processes for the production of plants are not patentable. Technical processes such as irradiation of seeds are patentable.

Table 2.1 **Distinct, uniform, and stable criteria (EPC Rule 26(4)): definition of a plant variety**

Any plant grouping within a single botanical taxon of the lowest known rank, which grouping, *irrespective of whether the conditions for the grant of a plant variety right are fully met*, can be:

- distinct: defined by the expression of the characteristics that result from a given genotype or combination of genotypes
- uniform: distinguished from any other plant grouping by the expression of at least one of the said characteristics
- stable: considered as a unit with regard to its suitability for being propagated unchanged.

Figure 2.8 An example related to plant breeders' rights

US 20040025209P1

(19) **United States**

(12) **Plant Patent Application Publication** (10) **Pub. No.: US 2004/0025209 P1**

Olesen et al. (43) **Pub. Date: Feb. 5, 2004**

(54) **MINIATURE ROSE VARIETY 'POULMONA'**

(50) Latin Name: ***Rosa hybrida***
Varietal Denomination: **POULMONA**

(76) Inventors: **L. Pernille Olesen**, Fredensborg (DK); **Mogens N. Olesen**, Fredensborg (DK)

Correspondence Address:
POULSEN ROSER APS
620 S. FRONT STREET
CENTRAL POINT, OR 97502 (US)

(21) Appl. No.: **10/211,119**

(22) Filed: **Aug. 2, 2002**

Publication Classification

(51) **Int. Cl.⁷** **A01H 5/00**
(52) **U.S. Cl.** **PLT/116**

(57) **ABSTRACT**

A new miniature rose which has large, deep pink flowers and attractive foliage. The variety successfully propagates from softwood cuttings and is suitable for year round production in commercial glasshouses. This new and distinct variety has shown to be uniform and stable in the resulting generations from asexual propagation.

Transgenic plants (basically these are plants where biotechnological modification "by human intervention" occurred) can only be patented in Europe:

- if the invention is applicable to make more than a particular plant variety
- if the plant grouping is not a variety, e.g. no individual plant varieties are mentioned in the claim.

Whether conventional, non-transgenic plant groupings obtained by breeding are also patentable in Europe is currently questioned.

Plant variety protection in the European Union is covered by regulation 2100/94/EC and based on the 1991 UPOV convention. CPVRs enable applicants to be granted a single IP right which is valid in all EU member states (not in selected individual countries). CPVRs are issued by the Community Plant Variety Office in France. Since the start of the CPVO in 1995, 41,059 applications had been filed up to the end of 2011. Most are related to ornamental plants (Figure 2.9).

Figure 2.9 CPVO applications, 1995–2011

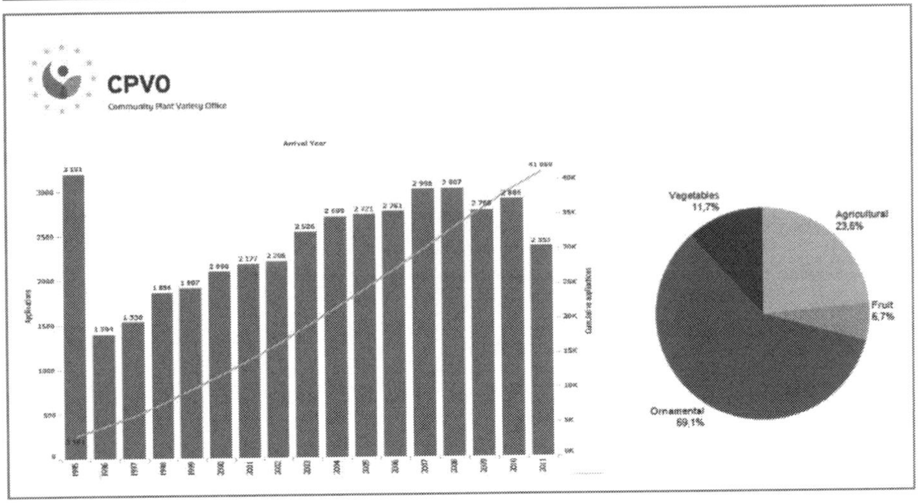

Source: CPVO.

Inventorship

Inventorship is not a criterion for invalidating a patent in Europe, but it is in the United States.

In Europe any natural person, company, or organization can apply for a patent under Article 58 of the European Patent Convention (EPC). EPC Article 60 refers to the inventor to whom a patent "can" be granted, but states that it is actually the applicant who is deemed to have the rights. Nevertheless, the inventor has the right to be mentioned on the patent and the moral right of paternity (EPC Article 62), but s/he can transfer the rights via an agreement, by inheritance, or as a consequence of being an employee.

Determination of inventorship can be a difficult task that requires legal analysis. "Conception" of the invention is typically considered the key for determining inventorship. Conception is the mental formulation and disclosure by the inventor(s) of a complete idea for a product or process. Contributions of labor or supervision are typically insufficient to get inventorship rights in the invention. In an academic setting it is often discretionary to name contributors to a research project in published articles. However, naming inventors on a patent application is not discretionary. If the inventorship on an issued patent is incorrect, a US court can invalidate the patent. Vice versa, if a person who contributed to the invention is not named as an inventor, a US court can invalidate the patent as well.

Until 16 March 2013, according to the AIA, the USPTO granted a US patent to the person who first invented (first-to-invent system). Most other countries (and also the United States after 16 March 2013) award the patent to the first to apply (first-to-file system). In either case, when pursuing patent protection one should ideally file a patent application as soon as the invention is complete. An invention is considered to be complete after it is conceived and reduced to practice. In the United States and some other jurisdictions, however, inventors can disclose their invention within one year before filing as US patent application and thus can rely on the so-called "grace period". The first-to-invent system in the United States should thus rather be read as the first-inventor-to-file principle. Indeed, if inventor A discloses his invention X before inventor B discloses the same invention X, inventor A can still apply for a US patent within a year after disclosing his invention, whereas inventor B cannot apply any more as his invention is anticipated by the disclosure of inventor A. It should further be clear that in the latter situation both inventors cannot obtain patent protection in – for example – Europe, as they both disclosed their invention before applying for a patent.

Conception is an inventor's mental formulation and disclosure of a complete idea for a product or process. The test for conception is whether the inventor's idea is definite and permanent enough for a person skilled in the art to understand the invention. Completion of an invention's second requirement, reduction to practice, has two stages: "constructive" and "actual". Filing a complete patent application satisfies "constructive" reduction to practice. To prove "actual" reduction to practice, an inventor must have:

- constructed a tangible form of the invention
- tested the device or process so as to demonstrate its capacity to perform its intended purpose successfully.

After conception, it is important that the inventor acts diligently to reduce an invention to practice and file a patent application.

The patent application

Patent protection is very important for the competitive advantage of companies. Several types of strategies can be followed. It can be offensive or defensive. The main approaches are presented in Table 2.2.

In advance of filing a regular patent application (mainly in the United States), an inventor has the option to file a provisional application to preserve for one year an early filing date. The requirements for filing a provisional application include a description, drawing figures (if necessary for understanding the invention), the official filing fee, and the name and home residence of each inventor. A provisional patent application is not examined, and can be converted into a non-provisional application at any time during this one-year period. In addition, an applicant has one year from the filing date to file any foreign patent applications claiming priority to the provisional patent application filing date. During this period more data can be added, provided that they support what is mentioned in the provisional application but do not expand it. The benefits of a provisional application are lower cost, the right to an earlier effective filing date, and minimal filing requirements. Provisional patent applications remain confidential (and a potential trade secret) if the applicant decides not to pursue a patent.

An inventor can choose to file immediately (if possible) a regular patent. A regular or non-provisional US patent application must provide the following specifications.

Table 2.2 Patent protection strategies

Single shot	Filing a simple patent that protects the invention as well as possible from different angles. Often used due to budget restrictions.
Blanketing	Numerous patents covering all aspects of an invention in a systematic way.
Flooding	A less structured approach where smaller areas fill the IP space around an invention, often using multiple smaller patents.
Surrounding	A first, broad patent is filed for an invention, followed by several smaller ones covering related aspects around the invention.
Combination into patent networks	Systematic building of a portfolio of different patents related to a specific area to get broad protection and a good position for negotiations.

- Describe the invention in sufficient detail to show a person skilled in the art that the inventor possessed the claimed invention at the time of filing ("written description requirement").
- Describe the invention in a manner that would allow one skilled in the art to make and use the claimed invention without additional experimentation ("enablement requirement").
- Disclose the best possible way to carry out the claimed invention at the time the application is filed ("best mode requirement").

The description must conclude with one or more claims that particularly and distinctly point out the novel subject matter of the invention. Drawings are "necessary for the understanding of the subject to be patented". Finally, the application must include an oath or declaration naming the true and correct inventors, and attach the required filing fee.

An applicant can follow two pathways, national or international, via the PCT. An overview of both pathways and related timings is presented in Figure 2.10. Note that a third pathway exists: a regional one, as for example governed by the EPC.

Ownership/applicant

In most countries both natural persons and corporations/organizations may apply for a patent. In most European countries ownership of an invention passes from the inventor to his/her employer by rule of law if the invention was made in the course of the inventor's normal or

Figure 2.10 Two possible pathways for patent application and related timings

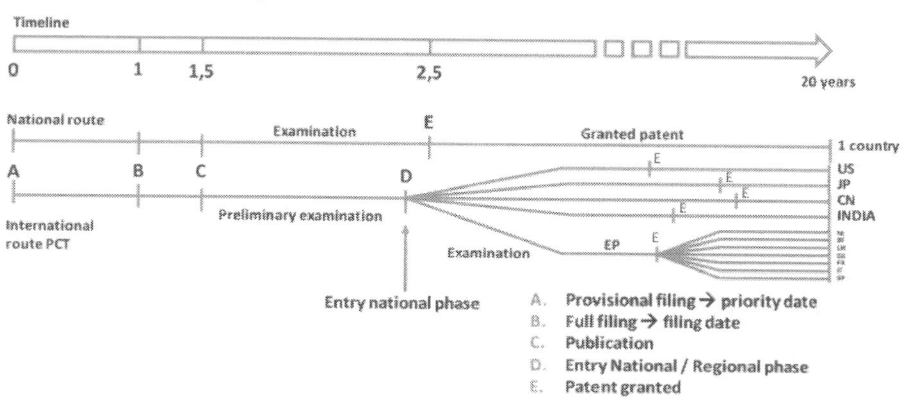

specifically assigned employment duties, where an invention might reasonably be expected to result from carrying out those duties, or if the inventor had a special obligation related to the interests of the employer's company.

The inventors, their successors, or their assignees become the proprietors of the patent when and if it is granted. If a patent is granted to more than one proprietor, the laws of the country in question and any agreement between the proprietors may affect the extent to which each proprietor can exploit the patent. For example, in some countries each proprietor may freely license or assign his/her rights in the patent to another person, while the law in other countries prohibits such actions without the permission of the other proprietor(s).

The ability to assign ownership rights increases the liquidity of a patent as property. Inventors can obtain patents and then sell them to third parties, just like any other asset. The third parties then own the patents, and have the same rights to prevent others from exploiting the claimed inventions as if they had originally made the inventions themselves. More details are given in Chapter 6 on valorization.

Specification and description

A patent for a new invention is requested by filing a written application at the relevant patent office. The person or company filing the application is referred to as "the applicant". The applicant may be the inventor or his/her assignee.

It is important to describe clearly and in detail the invention in relation to the claims. You must describe the claimed invention in such a manner that a person of ordinary skill in the application's technical field would understand and be capable of carrying out the claimed invention. In addition, the specification should describe as many alternate embodiments of the invention as reasonably possible in order to avoid any rejections by the patent office for lack of adequate description.

In some countries there are requirements for providing specific information such as the usefulness of the invention, the best mode of performing the invention known to the inventor (United States only), or the technical problem(s) solved by the invention. Drawings illustrating the invention may also be provided, if they are needed to describe it.

The enablement requirement states that the specification, at the time the application is filed, should describe the invention in such a manner that a person of ordinary skill in the art could make and use the claimed invention without additional, novel experimentation. The fact that a person of ordinary skill in the art is required to perform some experimentation when carrying out the claimed invention does not mean that such experimentation is "undue". However, the quality or quantity of this experimentation must not be unreasonable or unduly cumbersome.

To satisfy the best mode requirement, a US patent application at the time of filing must describe the inventor's preferred way of carrying out the claimed invention. This requirement is subjective, because it is dependent on the inventor's state of mind and not necessarily on whether the description provides the true best mode of carrying out the invention. The best mode requirement is intended to prevent the inventor(s) from concealing a preferred embodiment of the invention from the public. Thus if the inventor knows of a better way of carrying out the claimed invention and conceals it at the time of the application's filing, s/he fails to satisfy the best mode requirement and the patent will not be granted. However, the AIA indicates that failure to meet the best mode requirement cannot be used by third parties as a means to invalidate a patent.

For cost reasons (see below), it is also recommended to keep the description as short as possible to avoid high translation costs during the national phase.

After filing, a US application is often referred to as "patent pending". While this term does not confer legal protection, and a patent cannot be enforced until granted, it serves to give warning to potential infringers that if the patent is issued they may be liable for damages. It is also a nice "marketing tool". In contrast, a European patent application gives, after publication, the same rights in a designated contracting state as a granted patent, albeit provisionally.

For a patent to be granted, meaning that it is legally honored in a particular country, the application must meet the patentability requirements of that country. Most patent offices examine applications for compliance with these requirements. If an application does not comply, objections are communicated to the applicant or his/her patent agent or attorney, after which the applicant has one or more opportunities to respond to the objections to bring the application into compliance.

Claims

The application also includes one or more claims, although it is not always a requirement to submit these when first filing the application. The claims set out what the applicant is seeking to protect, in that they define what the patent owner will have a right to exclude others from making, using, or selling, depending on the case. In other words, the claims define what a patent covers or the "scope of protection".

When possible, it is recommended to be as broad as possible to cover the invention and further derivatives thereof. An example can be found in the patent filed on the use of endoperoxides for the treatment of flaviviridae such as hepatitis C and classic swine fever (US7842719B granted on 30 November 2010). "Serendipitously" the inventors found that artemisinin and derivatives (currently used for the treatment of malaria) had a good effect against various flaviviruses due to the actual endoperoxide moiety/functional group (Figure 2.11). They made their claims in this patent broad enough to cover other molecules containing this endoperoxide group (Figure 2.12).

This approach is often referred to as Markush claims, named after the first inventor to use this strategy.[1]

Innovative companies in the field of biomedicine will actively seek patent protection for biological products such as polypeptides they have developed, and try to commercialize these. In addition, protection will be sought for, if possible, methods to produce these biological products, and for their precursors, intermediates, variants, fragments... Examples of the latter are nucleic acids encoding polypeptides, vectors containing

Figure 2.11 Artemisinin with the endoperoxide functional group

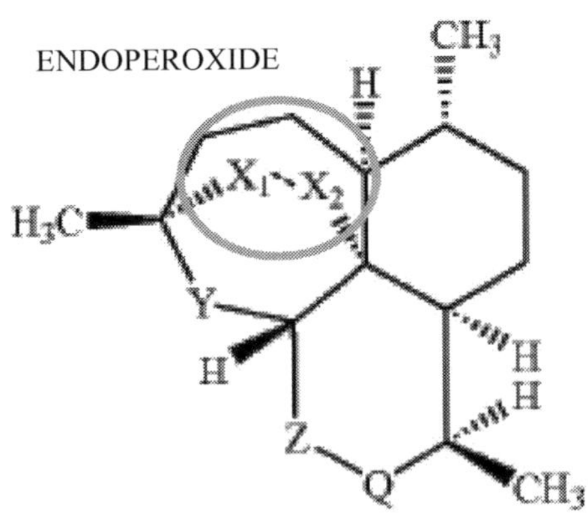

Figure 2.12 **Claims expanding the use of artemisinin to other compounds having an endoperoxide**

We claim:

1. A method of treating an infection caused by Flaviviridae sp.; comprising the step of administering an effective amount of a sesquiterpene having the formula:

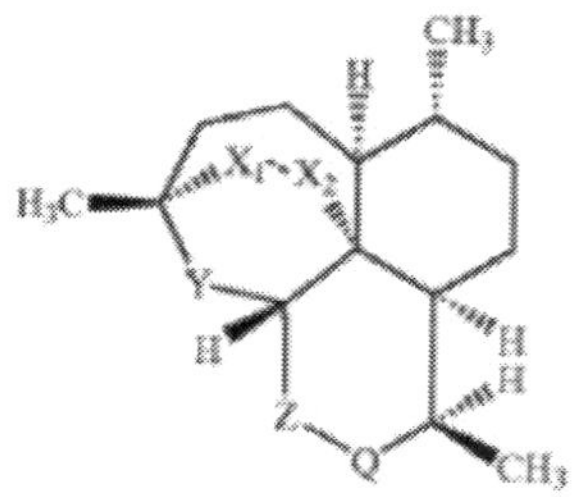

Wherein:

X1 and X2 are O;

Y is O;

Z is O, and

Q is selected from the group consisting of CO, CHOH, $CHOCH_3$, $CHOC_2H_5$, $CHOC_3H_7$, and $CHOCOCCH_2CH_2COOH$,

and the pharmaceutically acceptable salts thereof; and wherein the infection is hepatitis C or bovine viral diarrhea.

2. The method as defined in claim 1, wherein the infection is hepatitis C.
3. The method according to claim 2, wherein the sesquiterpene is administered in combination with interferon or peginterferon.

said nucleic acids, host cells containing said vectors, and homologues and fragments comprising bioactive regions of said polypeptides. Also methods wherein these products are used – such as methods to treat certain diseases – will be protected if allowed by patent law. Claims covering "methods to treat a disease" are patentable in the United States according to US patent law, but not within Europe according to European law. Claims to nucleic acids as such might not be patentable any more in the United States (discussed later).

In short, companies and their patent attorneys will often try to cover every aspect of their inventions in terms of broadly defined processes and products. Figure 2.13 shows two examples of patent applications in the field of biomedicine claiming polypeptides to treat certain diseases and/or methods to treat diseases via administering these polypeptides. The first example concerns one PCT application of the >500 patents and/or patent applications of the Belgian company Ablynx, which focuses on the development of antibody-derived therapeutic molecules. The second example concerns one US application of the >18,000 patents and/or patent applications of the US company Genentech (currently belonging to the Roche group), which conducts research in the areas of oncology, immunology, neuroscience, metabolism, and infectious disease.

Making claims too broad is also not recommended, because the patent examiner can decide that there are multiple inventions (there is no "unity" of invention) which all need to be filed separately, or the claims may be so broad that they encompass the prior art and are thus not patentable.

Costs

Some of the costs associated with obtaining a patent are the immediate costs for preparing the application and further prosecution, fees required by the patent offices, legal costs in prosecuting alleged infringements, business costs associated with those legal actions, costs relating to determining whether a method or product is covered by an existing patent (i.e. freedom to operate), translation costs, annual fees, etc.

The costs of preparing and filing a patent application, prosecuting it until grant, and maintaining the patent vary from one country to another, and may also be dependent upon the type and complexity of the invention and on the type of patent.

Obtaining and maintaining a patent can be very expensive. Therefore one should always ask the question, "Are the related market and expected sales high enough to justify the costs of a patent?" The initial costs are not too bad: €5,000–7,500 for drafting the patent and filing it at a patent office. From the PCT phase onwards it becomes more expensive (€7,000), but the costs really increase from the national phase onwards, e.g. filing in the United States costs approximately US$3,500, and similar for Japan and Europe. On top of that you have to include the cost of translations, if needed (US$0.12–0.38 per word), prosecution costs, and yearly annuities (US$200–5,000).

A decade ago the EPO estimated that the average cost of obtaining a European patent (via a Euro-direct application, i.e. not based on a PCT application) was around €31,000 (Roland Berger Market Research, 2004). This is approximately ten times more than in the United States. Since the London Agreement (a patent-related agreement signed on 17 October 2000 and aimed at reducing the translation costs of European

Figure 2.13 A: Example of a biomedical patent application for Ablynx, including the first "product" claim (claim 1) and the first "method" claim (claim 26) of a total of 50 claims; B: Example of a biomedical patent application for Genentech, including the first "method" claim (claim 1 of a total of 25 claims)

A

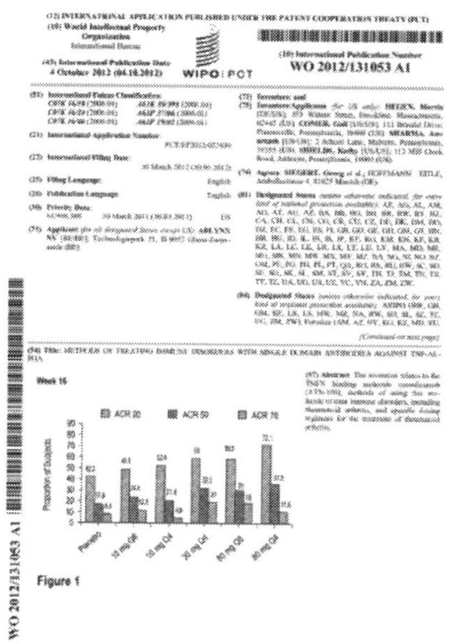
WO 2012/131053 A1

Figure 1

1) A polypeptide comprising two anti-tumor necrosis factor alpha (TNFa) SDABs and an anti-human serum albumin (HSA) SDAB for use in treating an immune disorder in a human in need thereof, by administering to the human multiple 30–400 mg doses of said polypeptide, wherein the doses are at least about every four weeks apart.

B

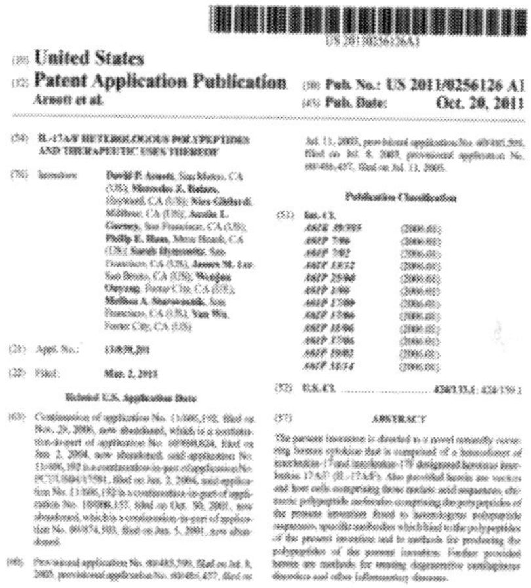
United States
Patent Application Publication
Pub. No.: US 2011/0256126 A1
Pub. Date: Oct. 20, 2011

ABSTRACT

1) A method of treating an immune-related disorder in a mammal in need thereof, comprising administering to said mammal a therapeutically effective amount of one or more antagonists capable of inhibiting both IL-17A (SEQ ID NO: 3) and IL-17F (SEQ ID NO: 4) in an IL-17A/F polypeptide.

patents granted under the EPC) entered into force on 1 May 2008, however, this estimation is no longer up to date, since fewer translations are required (EPO, 2008). Up-to-date fees for EPO and PCT filings can be found on the EPO website.

The unitary Community patent will of course further reduce the cost of patenting in Europe. After 40 years of debate the European Parliament signed an agreement on 11 December 2012 regarding a unitary patent, which may come into force in mid-2015 at the earliest. Until then, a granted European patent needs to be validated at a national level, resulting in a costly procedure due to registration requirements and translations in each member state. Under the new unitary regime, applicants will have, in addition to the existing system of national validation, the option to apply for a patent valid in 25 of the 28 member states. Accompanying the unitary patent will be the new Unified Patent Court, which will have jurisdiction for litigation relating not only to unitary patents but also to European patents validated in member states in the "classical way". However, during a transition period applicants for and owners of classical European patents will be permitted to opt out of the Unified Patent Court and have any infringement or invalidity proceedings dealt with at a national level, as in the past.

Once granted, a patent is subject in most countries to renewal fees to keep it in force. These are generally payable on a yearly basis. Some countries and regional patent offices (e.g. the EPO) also require annual renewal fees to be paid for a patent application before it is granted. Renewal fees will also have to be paid to the EPO for a unitary patent.

Costs related to a patent filing include the cost of a patent attorney, payment of official filing fees, translations, and in-house expenses. During the lifetime of a patent annuities also need to be paid. Estimated total costs for the major markets, including annuities, are presented in Table 2.3.

For one approved patent filed in all major markets, the total cost during the patent lifespan can be estimated to be €200,000–250,000 (Figure 2.14).

The American Intellectual Property Law Association conducted a study in 2005, based on a survey of patent lawyers and court documents for a sample of 89 cases where one side was ordered to pay the other side's legal fees, to estimate the cost of patent litigation (AIPLA, 2005). It concluded that direct legal costs of patent litigation are on average in the order of $1 million per case, not including associated business costs. In a more recent study (AIPLA, 2011), details are provided on patent litigation costs in relation to the amount of money at stake. For a claim that could be worth less than US$1 million, average legal costs are $650,000. Between $1 million and $25 million the total litigation costs can reach $2.5 million. For a claim over $25 million, average legal costs are $5 million.

Table 2.3 Global estimated IP costs for the major markets

Country	Total estimated costs (US$)
Brazil	21,135
Canada	12,733
China	18,780
European Union	11,541
India	12,421
Japan	31,565
Korea	29,230
Mexico	14,879
Norway	22,532
Russian Federation	19,783
Singapore	12,026
South Africa	6,945
Switzerland	16,126
Taiwan	15,551
Turkey	22,370
United States	11,130

Source: de Vuyst (2006).

Figure 2.14 The lifespan of a patent and accumulated costs

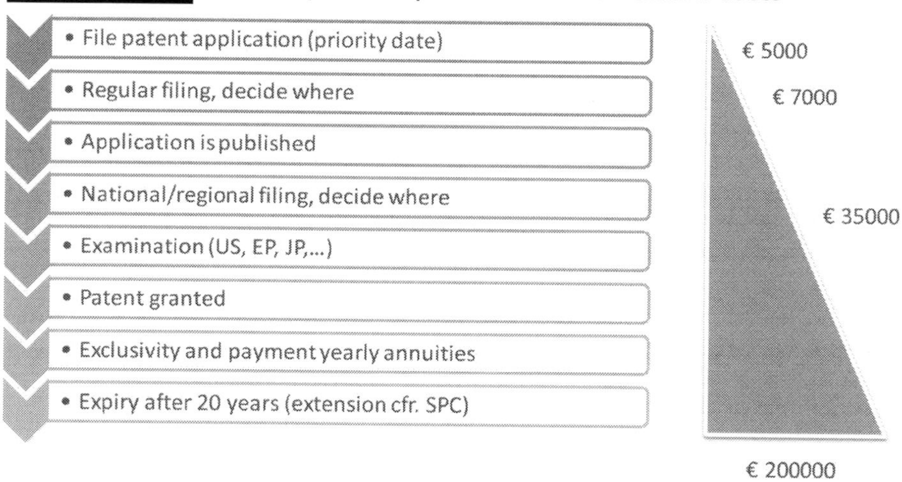

Continuing applications

US patent law allows applicants to file continuing patent applications claiming the benefit of the disclosure and filing date of an earlier filed co-pending application ("parent application"). The parent application does not have to be the first or earliest filed application in a chain of continuing applications; it just has to be a related application that is co-pending at the time of filing. Continuing applications must share at least one common inventor with the parent application, make a specific claim of priority to the parent application, and be filed while the parent application is co-pending. Although continuing applications claim the benefit of the earlier filed "parent" application, they are newly filed applications that restart the examination process.

There are three types of continuing patent applications recognized in US patent practice:

- continuation applications
- continuation-in-part applications
- divisional applications.

Continuation applications have the same specification as the parent application, but with different claims. Continuation applications are useful to:

- claim subject matter that was disclosed but not fully claimed in the parent application
- seek broader or different claim coverage
- present new arguments to support allowance of the application after a final rejection is received or prosecution is closed
- keep an application pending to capture developments not specifically addressed by any of the issued claims.

A continuation-in-part application is one in which the inventor provides substantially the same specification as in the parent patent application, but discloses additional information that was not included in the parent application.

Divisional applications can be filed in response to an office action from the USPTO stating that the claims of the parent application are directed to two or more distinct inventions (e.g. claims to a product and claims to a method of making it can be considered distinct inventions). Divisional applications, but not continuation or continuation-in-part applications, can also be filed with the EPO.

Requirements

There are some differences between US and EPC requirements for a patent, as shown in Table 2.4. The subtle differences are important when preparing a patent application, but are considered to be very similar/identical under Article 27 of TRIPS. "Specification" relates to the fact that the invention needs to be written in detail and must be mature (in the best possible way). The level of detail is also important in Europe (EPC Articles 83 and 84). "Utility" in the United States and "industrial applicability" in Europe are often referred to as "being commercial".

For many the difference between novel and non-obvious (in the United States) and inventive step (in Europe) is not clear. "Novel" is when something has not been disclosed before. "Non-obvious" is when the novel finding is the consequence of someone skilled in the art combining different existing technologies in a non-straightforward manner. Something is thus obvious if in the past predictions have been made regarding possible future applications of the existing technology. The EPO uses the so-called "problem-and-solution approach" to determine if an invention involves an "inventive step". The latter method involves determination of the closest prior art; formulation of the objective technical problem; and determining whether there is any teaching in the prior art as a whole that would – not could – have prompted a skilled person, faced with the objective technical problem, to modify or adapt the closest prior art, thereby achieving what the invention achieves.

As mentioned earlier, for something to be patentable, in general it must be:

- a patentable subject matter = an invention = a technical solution to a problem
- new or novel

Table 2.4 Requirements for patentability

Europe	United States
Novelty	Utility
Inventive step	Novelty
Industrial applicability	Non-obviousness
Subject not part of the list of exceptions	Specification

- useful (United States), with an objective, global demand; or susceptible to industrial application (Europe)
- non-obvious, or inventive, or not easily derivable from what is already known
- best mode (United States).

An overview of subjects that can or cannot be patented under European patent law (see EPC Articles 52 and 53) is presented in Figure 2.15.

A "process" is a way to make or use a product. For example, a process can consist of mixing fruits with yoghurt at a certain temperature to produce a smoothie. Not all processes are patentable.

Under US law, it is generally agreed that more subject matter is patentable, and it is sometimes said that "anything under the sun that is made by man is patentable". However, in the United States there are also exceptions, including:

- laws of nature
- unethical or immoral subjects
- natural phenomena
- abstract ideas.

Figure 2.15 What can and cannot be patented under European patent law

What can be patented?

YES

1. A product
2. The apparatus for producing the product
3. The process for producing the product
4. The use of the product

NO

1. Computer programs
2. Medical and surgical treatments
3. Mathematical methods
4. Business methods (but changing, TRIPS)
5. Discoveries
6. Aesthetic creations
7. New variety of plant or animal
8. Inventions which are contrary to moral standards and public order (e.g. instruments of torture)
9. The human body and any non-separate part(s) thereof

In this regard, the US Supreme Court recently (June 2013) decided in a patent case concerning the so-called BRCA genes (*Association for Molecular Pathology v. Myriad Genetics*) that "naturally" occurring nucleic acids, such as isolated BRCA genes, are "products of nature" and not patentable any more – only sequences different to those in nature, such as cDNA, are still patentable. In another recent US Supreme Court case (*Mayo Collaborative Services v. Prometheus Laboratories*) it was decided that processes solely describing a naturally occurring correlation (which is often the case in diagnostic assays correlating the occurrence of a specific biomarker with a certain disease) are natural phenomena and thus no longer patentable. Claims covering such a diagnostic assay should thus contain "more" than the natural principle itself! In other words, and at least in life sciences, it appears that not "anything under the sun that is made by man" is still patentable in the United States.

However, the new use or application of e.g. a species of plant or animal can be patented. For instance, researchers identified a type of butyric acid-producing strain and observed a very good effect on gastrointestinal health. On 23 February 2009 they filed a patent application titled "Method for alleviating intestinal problems and novel bacterial strains therefore" (WO2010/094789). The first two claims mentioned in the patent are:

- butyric acid-producing strains for use as a medicament characterized therein that the butyric acid-producing strains are chosen from *Butyricicoccus pullicaecorum* deposited at the public BCCM/LMG bacterial collection as *B. pullicaecorum* LMG24109 and strains showing at least 93 percent homology to the 16S rRNA sequence of *B. pullicaecorum* characterized by SEQ ID No 1
- butyric acid-producing strains according to claim 1 for use in the prophylaxis and/or treatment of intestinal health problems of humans and/or animals.

Notice that the claim was written broadly enough so that other related bacteria (>93 percent homology to the 16S rRNA sequence of the claimed strain *B. pullicaecorum*) are covered in the patent application.

Inventions may often encompass more than one category of patentable subject matter. Accordingly, patents will often have more than one type of claim.

For an invention to be patentable, it must be new or "novel" (i.e. not belonging to the prior art). If the prior art shows every element of a claim, the claim is unpatentable and is "anticipated" by the prior art. Rules regarding prior art differ around the world. In the United States prior art is "everything" in the public domain that existed before the date of filing the patent application except what is made available by the inventor within one year prior to the filing date. For most other countries, prior art is "everything" prior to the priority filing date of a patent application (i.e. most countries do not recognize a "one-year" grace period). For a patented invention to be rejected over a prior art reference, the reference must have been accessible somewhere in the world. Secret or non-public materials cannot be considered as prior art.

Publications, abstracts, websites, and interviews are all prior art, as is an invoice of a single sale!

Prior art can invalidate a patent. In Belgium, for instance, De Mayer and De Smet participated in a TV show called "The Inventors" in 2007 and filed a patent on gingerbread-based paste. The IP rights were purchased by the company Lotus NV, which started commercializing. Unfortunately, the exact formula had been available online (www.omawapsie.nl) since 2002. Thus the court of Ghent declared the patent invalid on 20 January 2011.

To meet the utility requirement, a patent application must also demonstrate that the claimed invention is "useful" for some purpose. In most technical fields this utility requirement has a low threshold which is easily satisfied by demonstrating any useful result. For a patented invention to fail to satisfy the utility requirement it must be "totally incapable of achieving a useful result", which is rare in applications for processes, machines, and products.

It is very important for any researcher or inventor to conduct an in-depth prior art analysis, preferably before starting work on a new project. The entire body of knowledge from the beginning of time to present prior art is a term used in patent law to describe broadly the literature, public domain, and existing patents which need to be studied (USLegal.com, undated). An overview of some areas and sources is presented in Table 2.5.

A patent is not granted if the invention was patented or described in a printed publication in a country, or is in public use or on sale. Furthermore, before commercializing a patent it is important to study the freedom to operate. FTO is the process of determining whether or not a product can be made, used, marketed, or sold without infringing another's valid, enforceable patent. Although this analysis is crucial before launching a product or process, it is also applicable

Table 2.5 Areas and sources to look for prior art

Literature/public domain	Patents
Web of science, databases	www.wipo.int
Current contents	www.uspto.gov
MedTrack	www.epo.org
Scientific journals	Espacenet.com
Trade journals	www.google.com/patents
Magazines	Thomsoninnovation.com (pay site)
Newspapers	www.pat2pdf.com
WWW	www.micropat.com (pay site)

to non-commercial activities such as research, since these activities can eventually lead to liability for patent infringements.

For instance, referring to the previous example on the use of artemisinin-related derivatives for the treatment of e.g. hepatitis C, before launching a possible new medication the active compound needs to be formulated for easy and efficient administration to patients. A broad FTO needs to be studied, since this formulation may use excipients that are patented by others, or it could be offered in a recipient/container that was patented by others, etc.

In conducting an obviousness analysis, an examiner may combine multiple prior art references. The examiner cannot, however, combine references arbitrarily. The non-obviousness rule requires that an examiner steps into the shoes of a person of ordinary skill at the time the invention was made and determines whether the claimed invention would have been obvious without using hindsight obtained by reviewing the patent application.

An invention is obvious if the differences between the material to be patented and the prior art are such that the invention as a whole would have been obvious at the time it was made to a person having ordinary skill in the art to which said subject matter pertains. Hence simply combining different existing technologies to produce an invention in such a manner as any person having ordinary skills could have done will most probably be considered obvious. It needs a non-straightforward, unique step ("1+1 must often be 3") in order to be non-obvious.

The level of "ordinary skill in the art" required of a hypothetical person is more than that of an ordinary person but less than that of a very creative expert in the field of the invention. Determining the level of skill in the art is a subtle matter that is often open to debate. Factors often considered in such a determination can include the level of sophistication in the technology, the education of an ordinary person in the field, and prior art attempts to solve related problems.

Courts may often refer to objective evidence of obviousness or non-obviousness as "secondary considerations". Such secondary considerations include a long-felt need for the invention, commercial success of the invention, and copying by others. For example, if there was a long need for the claimed solution to a problem, or if the invention is commercially successful, the claimed invention is more likely to be non-obvious. Also, showing that the prior art leads away from the claimed invention can be used to support non-obviousness.

Governing laws and prosecution

Granting and enforcing patents are governed by national laws, and by international treaties where those treaties have been taken up in national laws. Hence, patents are territorial in nature.

A key international treaty for patents is the Paris Convention for the Protection of Industrial Property, initially signed in 1883. The Paris Convention sets out a range of basic rules relating to patents; although it does not have direct legal effect in all countries, its principles are incorporated into all notable current patent systems. Its most significant aspect is the provision of the right to claim priority: filing an application in any one member state of the Paris Convention preserves the right for one year to file in any other member state and receive the benefit of the original filing date. Because eligibility for a patent is intensely date-driven, this right is fundamental to modern patent usage.

There is a trend towards global harmonization of patent laws, with the WTO being particularly active in this area. The TRIPS agreement of 1994 has been largely successful in providing a forum for nations to agree on an aligned set of patent laws. Conformity with the TRIPS agreement is a requirement of admission to the WTO, and so compliance is seen by many nations as important. This has led to many developing nations, which may historically have developed different laws according to their specific needs, enforcing patent laws in line with global practice.

In addition there are international treaty procedures, such as those under the EPO's EPC and WIPO's PCT covering more than 140 countries, that centralize some portion of the filing and examination process. In the United States, President Obama signed the new AIA in 2011, and on 11 December 2012 the EU Parliament signed an agreement for an EU unitary patent.

Some 148 countries currently honor the PCT, which permits applicants to file international patent applications. A PCT application may also be used to prove priority, without a patent ever being issued. Within 30 months from the priority date, the applicant must file individual patent applications in all countries in which examination is desired (i.e. PCT applications provide an additional 18 months in which to file foreign applications beyond the typical one-year "priority" period for filing foreign applications claiming "priority"). Filing a PCT application can be advantageous in the following respects.

- If an applicant is interested in filing a patent application in numerous countries, a PCT application gives the benefit of a PCT patent examiner's prior art search and results before incurring the expense of filing numerous applications.
- A PCT application gives an applicant additional time (30 months from the priority date) to delay the expenses associated with applying for patent protection in individual countries.
- Many countries give credence to a PCT examiner's search and opinion on patentability, which can limit the costs of pursuing a patent application in individual countries.

Rules for obtaining a patent differ from country to country. Patent protection in each country requires national filing, usually with the country's patent office. Most nations have signed the Paris Convention and permit applicants a non-extendible period of one year from the date of their priority filing (e.g. a US provisional patent application) to extend their patent application in other countries. If a "foreign" patent application is filed within this one-year period and claims priority to e.g. a US (provisional) patent application, the US filing date is the applicable priority date of the application.

Patents can generally only be enforced through civil lawsuits in the country where the infringement takes place. Typically, the assignee will seek monetary compensation for past infringement, and a ruling by a court to prohibit the defendant from engaging in future acts of infringement. To prove infringement, the assignee must establish that the accused infringer practices all the requirements of at least one of the claims of the patent.

Nevertheless, the vast majority of patent rights are not determined through litigation, but resolved privately through patent licensing. Patent licensing agreements are effectively contracts in which the patent owner (the licensor) agrees to forgo its right to sue the licensee for infringement of the licensor's patent rights, usually in return for a royalty or other compensation. It is common for companies engaged in complex technical fields to enter into dozens of license agreements associated with the production of a single product. Licensing is explained in more detail in Chapter 6.

Supplementary protection certificate

This certificate for additional protection is regulated in Europe via EC 1768/92 of 18 June 1992. It is for e.g. pharmaceutical-related patents. The SPC is covered in the United States by the Drug Price Competition and Patent Term Restoration Act of 1984.

An SPC comes into force only after the corresponding general patent expires. It normally has a maximum lifetime of five years, but the duration can be extended to 5.5 years in cases relating to a human medicinal product for which data from clinical trials conducted in accordance with an agreed principal investigator's plan (PIP) have been submitted.

The total combined duration of market exclusivity of a general patent and an SPC cannot normally exceed 15 years. A granted five-month SPC extension for the submission of data from an agreed PIP can extend this combined duration to 15.5 years. It is still unclear whether legally more than 15.5 years can be obtained in particular circumstances. An SPC extends the lifetime of a patent, but under somewhat different rights.

SPCs in Europe are based primarily upon two regulations. Although all European countries are required to provide SPCs, no uniform mutual recognition exists: applications must be filed and approved on a country-by-country basis.

Notes

1. Eugene Markush, US Patent No. 1.506.316, dated 26 August 1924.

Trade secrets

Abstract: Keeping information secret instead of disclosing it via filing – for example – a patent application can sometimes be a preferred manner to protect the economic value of this information. This chapter describes what a trade secret is, what should be done to keep information secret, and what the weaknesses of trade secrets are.

Key words: protecting trade secrets, reverse engineering.

What is a trade secret?

A trade secret is important information that a company keeps secret to give it a competitive advantage. The most famous trade secret is the Coca-Cola® formula.

Trade secrets are not protected by IP-related laws. Protection is achieved by keeping the information a secret and not disclosing it.

A trade secret can be a formula, sales-related info, business strategy, practice, process, design, instrument, pattern, or compilation of information that is not generally known or reasonably ascertainable by which a business can obtain an economic advantage over competitors or customers. In some jurisdictions such secrets are referred to as "confidential information" or "classified information".

Business law provides a mechanism for protecting proprietary and sensitive business information. A trade secret, by definition, is information that has economic value and is secret. There are no formal application requirements to obtain a trade secret. Unlike patents, there are no statutory requirements that a trade secret needs to be novel, useful, and non-obvious, and there is no examination process. Trade secret protection arises once the appropriate steps are taken to create and maintain a valid secret. Trade secrets are not subject to a predefined term, and can be maintained for an indefinite period as long as they are kept secret.

The precise language by which a trade secret is defined varies country by country, as do the particular types of information that are subject to trade secret protection. There are three criteria that are common to all such definitions:

- the secret is not generally known to the public
- there is an economic benefit for its holder
- adequate efforts are taken or a *modus operandi* is available to maintain its secrecy.

This broad definition means that nearly any type of business information can qualify as a trade secret. Hence, information that is not otherwise patentable can qualify. Some examples of information that can be protected as trade secrets are listed below.

- *Product and manufacturing related*
  - Computer programs.
  - Manufacturing processes.
  - Technical information.
  - Prototypes.
  - Formulas.
  - Product testing results (positive and negative).
  - Drawings.
  - Product ingredients (food, cosmetics, drugs, etc.).

- *Sales and marketing related*
  - Client identities.
  - Product pricing.
  - Customer lists.
  - Vendors.
  - Market analyses and strategies.

- *Company and business related*
  - Company manuals.
  - Financial statements.
  - Strategic plans.
  - Salaries and employee data.

Published information, such as that disclosed on the internet or in a book, magazine, trade magazines, website, or other media, cannot be maintained as a trade secret because it is "generally known" and readily available. This can be particularly important when deciding whether to keep information as a trade secret or pursue patent protection for that information. Anything disclosed in a patent after it is published is generally known and readily ascertainable, and cannot be protected as a trade secret.

The final and often most important criterion for a trade secret is that a company needs to have a *modus operandi* in place to protect the information and maintain its secrecy. Maintaining secrecy of a trade secret is viewed under a reasonable standard which does not require absolute secrecy.

A company can protect its confidential information through non-compete and non-disclosure contracts with its employees (within the constraints of employment law, including only restraint that is reasonable in terms of territory and time). The law of protection of confidential information effectively allows a perpetual monopoly in secret information – hence it does not expire as a patent would. The lack of formal protection means that a third party is not prevented from independently duplicating and using the secret information once it is discovered.

The sanctioned protection of such information from public disclosure is viewed as an important legal tool by which a society protects its overall economic strength. A company typically invests money, time, and labor in generating information regarding refinements of processes and operations. If competitors had access to the same knowledge, the first company's ability to survive or maintain its market dominance or market position and market share would be jeopardized. Where trade secrets are recognized, the creator of knowledge regarded as a "trade secret" is entitled to regard such "special knowledge" as intellectual property.

A court considers several factual inquiries when considering reasonable secrecy.

- Whether employees have executed confidentiality or non-disclosure agreements.
- Whether the company's confidentiality policy is set down in writing, e.g. via an SOP.
- Whether access to the trade secret is limited to essential employees/ contractors.

- Whether employees who have access to the trade secret are aware that it is to be maintained as a secret, e.g. clearly stating "confidential" on related documents.
- Whether the information is kept in a restricted area such as a locked file, within security-encrypted software, in a restricted location within a physical plant, etc.
- Whether documents containing information that is trade secret are properly labeled.
- Whether the company actively screens employee publications and presentations for disclosure of trade secret information.

A poor, non-explicit intent to keep information secret, without affirmative acts, is typically insufficient to maintain a trade secret.

Protection of trade secrets can, in principle, extend indefinitely and therefore may provide an advantage over patent protection, which lasts only for a specific period of time (20 years). Coca-Cola, for example, has no patent for its formula and has been very effective in guarding it for far longer than the 20 years of protection a patent would have provided. In fact, Coca-Cola refused to reveal its trade secret under at least two judges' orders. The disadvantage is that there is no protection once information kept as a trade secret is uncovered by others through reverse engineering, for example, whereas a patent gives a guaranteed period of protection in exchange for disclosing the information to the public.

Protecting trade secrets

Trade secrets are by definition not disclosed to the world at large. Instead, their owners seek to keep their special knowledge out of the hands of competitors through a variety of civil and commercial means, not the least of which is the use of non-disclosure agreements (NDAs or CDAs) and non-compete clauses, as described in Chapter 1. In exchange for an opportunity to be employed by the holder of secrets, a worker may sign an agreement not to reveal his or her prospective employer's proprietary information. An employee may also surrender or assign to the employer the right to his/her own intellectual work produced during the course or as a condition of employment. Violation of the agreements generally carries the possibility of heavy financial penalties, which operate as a disincentive to reveal trade secrets.

For instance, in March 2011 FoodManufacture reported that in the UK Goldenfry Foods had won a legal judgment against three former employees who misused trade secrets to establish a breakaway company and appropriate a £5 million supermarket contract for gravy granules (Bouckley, 2011). The three co-defendants and the company they owned, Frontiers Foods, faced a multimillion bill for damages and legal costs as a result of revealing/using this trade secret. It was a long and difficult case. Employees cannot take trade secrets to another firm, but they can take enhanced skills and knowledge. There is often a thin line between these. Finally, the court was convinced of the fact that the three former employees misused the trade secret since they had left in January and only three months later secured the large deal: it is highly unlikely that someone could do this in such a short time period from scratch.

A holder of a trade secret may also require similar agreements from other parties it deals with, such as vendors or licensees.

In the United States and also often other jurisdictions the court defines misappropriation of a trade secret as:

- acquisition of a trade secret of another by a person who knows or has reason to know that the trade secret was acquired by improper means
- disclosure or use of a trade secret of another without express or implied consent by a person who:
  - used improper means to acquire knowledge of the trade secret
  - at the time of disclosure or use knew or had reason to know that this knowledge of the trade secret was:
    - derived from or through a person who has utilized improper means to acquire it
    - acquired under circumstances giving rise to a duty to maintain its secrecy or limit its use
    - derived from or through a person who owed a duty to the person seeking relief to maintain its secrecy or limit its use
  - before a material change of his/her position, knew or had reason to know that it was a trade secret and that knowledge of it had been acquired by accident or mistake.

Again, when a company discloses a trade secret to others, such as employees, manufacturers, suppliers, consultants, etc., those disclosures should be made under a written duty of confidentiality. This is typically done by requiring the party to execute a CDA or NDA, or by way of an employment contract or a third-party consulting or supplier agreement.

If a party under a duty of confidentiality to the trade secret owner breaches that duty, the owner's enforcement effort will benefit from a written agreement that clearly recognizes the trade secret status of the information.

Reverse engineering of trade secrets

Under patent law, a subsequent inventor can be liable even though the invention was developed completely independently and without knowledge of the patented invention. Under trade secret law, independent discovery and use of the trade secret are not a violation.

Companies often try to discover one another's trade secrets through lawful methods of reverse engineering on one hand, and potentially unlawful methods including industrial espionage on the other. Acts of industrial espionage are generally illegal in their own right under the relevant governing laws. The importance of that illegality to trade secret law is as follows: if a trade secret is acquired by improper means, the secret is generally deemed to have been misappropriated. Thus if a trade secret has been obtained via industrial espionage, its acquirer will probably be subject to legal liability for acquiring it improperly. The paramount condition is of course that the owner of the trade secret has a solid system in place to protect the secret. Therefore it is of crucial importance to evaluate whether a product (or process) is easy to be reverse engineered. If yes, the trade secret pathway is most probably not the best and it could be better to consider applying for a patent.

The acquisition of a known product must, of course, also be by a fair and honest means, such as purchase of the item on the open market, for reverse engineering to be lawful... Thus discovery of another's trade secret requires proper acquisition of the information and ethical business practices.

Giving detailed examples or case studies regarding trade secrets is not that easy, simply because companies and people keep and need to keep secrets safe. Nevertheless, we want to provide a strategic related example, without supplying too much detail.

In 2010 researchers at Ghent University discovered and developed a new system to protect omega-3 fatty acids from rumen degradation so that more of these fatty acids could be deposited in milk. The system and product were new, but prior art could be found on most of the different parts of the system, making it rather difficult to get a patent granted due to problems with non-obviousness. Nevertheless, the final product was extremely complex, making reverse engineering very difficult. Furthermore, the product needs to be produced via a difficult and very specific process. For these reasons, the invention was kept as a trade secret and no patent application was filed, since it was unlikely that it would be granted. What is more, the trade secret could be lost if the patent application was published.

4

Trademarks

Abstract: In daily life we come across numerous different trademarks, which are another form of registered intellectual property. This chapter defines the different forms of trademarks. It also describes how you can create and register your own trademark – it is not as difficult as people sometimes tend to believe. In addition, some related forms of IP are presented, such as protected geographical status in the European Union and domain names for websites.

Key words: trademark, registration, protection, domain names, PGS.

What is a trademark?

A trademark is a name, sign, or indicator used by an individual, business organization, or other legal entity to identify itself or its products/services in the market as being different from others.

A typical trademark/logo is presented in Figure 4.1. Food2Know is a consortium of scientists conducting research on the complete food chain, from farm to fork. Since Food2Know relates to a consortium, it is actually more a collective mark (see below).

Use of symbols or signatures to identify the source of goods has been around ever since people first started trading and selling things like pottery, weapons, and clothing thousands of years ago. Blacksmiths in the Roman Empire used a symbol to mark their craft. These were a first form of trademark. Another old trademark is Stella Artois, which claims use since 1366.

Figure 4.1 The trade name Food2Know and its logo

According to the OECD (2010), the number of trademarks a country or company registers/uses is a possible measure to assess the level of innovation of that country or company (Figure 4.2).

Figure 4.2 Trademarks per capita for the period 2005–2007

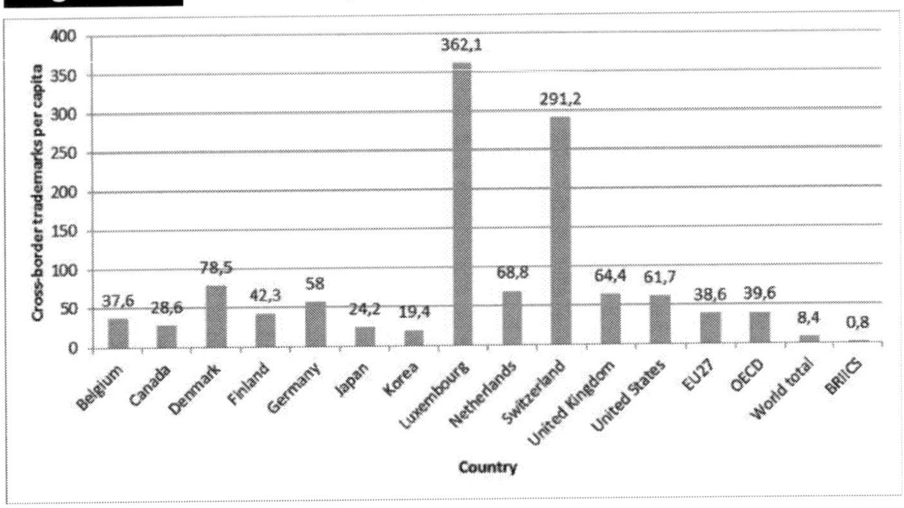

Source: Based on OECD (2009).

In some jurisdictions, e.g. the United States, a trademark can be designated by different symbols, depending on if it is registered or not:

™ for an unregistered product/name trademark
℠ for an unregistered service mark
® for a registered trademark.

The use of these symbols is not mandatory in other jurisdictions.

A trademark is typically a name, word, logo, symbol, design, image, or a combination of these elements. There is also a range of non-conventional trademarks that do not fall into these standard categories, and make use of rather peculiar differentiators such as color, smell, or sound.

Trademark, trade name, and company name

It is important to understand the difference between a trademark, a trade name, and a company name. A trademark is a sign used by an entity to identify the origin of its goods or services in the market. A trade name is the name used by a company to identify itself in the market. A company name is the name of the company according to its statutes. In some cases a company name, its trade name, and its trademark are the same. A typical example is Coca-Cola. In other cases the company name and trade name are completely different from the trademarks owned by that company. Unilever, for example, has a portfolio of 500+ trademarks for different products it offers to the market.

Table 4.1 notes some of the key features of different types of signs. It is common for people to lump all these terms together as trademarks. Trademarks are also often referred to as brands.

Trademarks serve to identify a particular undertaking as the origin of goods or services – this is known as trademark use. Certain exclusive rights attach to a registered mark and can be enforced by way of an action for trademark infringement, while unregistered trademark rights may be enforced based on the governing laws of a specific country. The proprietor of a registered trademark is entitled to prevent all third parties not having its consent from using identical or similar signs in the course of trade. In most cases the proprietor will have to prove that there is a likelihood of confusion by the public between the trademark and the sign.

Table 4.1 Classification of trademark types of signs

Type of mark	Key features
Word mark Coca-Cola	If the sign consists only of a word
Graphical mark	When the sign has a certain graphical representation
Color mark	If the sign is a color or combination of different colors, e.g. the purple of Milka Lila products
Collective mark FAIRTRADE	Sign used by members of a cooperative, association, or other collective group or organization to indicate membership, e.g. Food2Know, Fairtrade, etc.
Shape mark 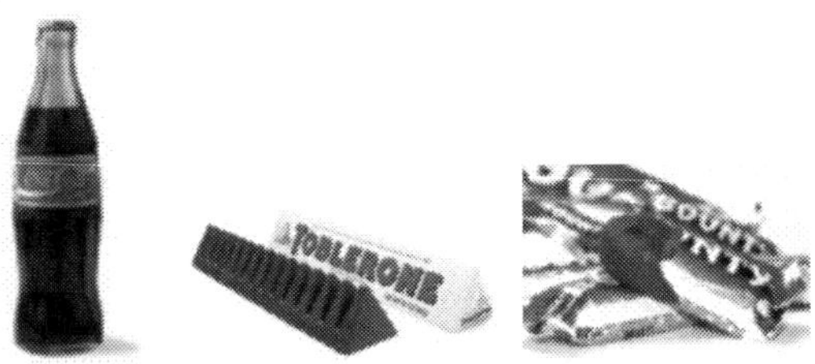 	Sign for which the shape can be recognized by consumers as originating from a certain company
Sound mark 	If the sign is a sound, e.g. the roaring lion of MGM
Complex/combination marks	When the sign consists of different type of marks, e.g. word/graphical

It is important that a trademark is capable of distinguishing goods and services of one business from those of others (to have distinctive power). Furthermore, it must be capable of graphical representation and must be put to use for those goods or services for which it is registered.

Developing a trademark

Selecting the right trademark for a product is of crucial importance, as it can make the difference between success and failure of the product. Brand management needs to consider both legal and business aspects. The primary legal consideration is the selection of the strongest trademark possible (Figure 4.3).

Generic designations cannot be registered or protected because they are incapable of functioning as a differentiator or source indicator. A word can be inherently generic, such as the word "beer".

Next on the scale of protection are "merely descriptive" words that simply describe the product or convey an immediate idea of what it does, e.g. cherry beer. Because descriptive signs simply describe a product, they cannot be registered or protected unless and until they acquire distinctive character in the marketplace through use. The process of acquiring distinctive character is called *inburgering* (there is no English word for this).

In addition, non-traditional trademarks such as sound, color, and scent are not protected until they acquire secondary meaning, e.g. the typical Nokia ringtone. This is because consumers do not see them as an indicator of the origin of the goods or service straight away. That process takes time and marketing efforts.

Suggestive marks are next on the scale of protection, and require some imagination, thought, or perception to come to a conclusion as to the exact nature of the goods.

Figure 4.3 The strength of a trademark

The most distinctive marks on the scale are those that are either entirely *de novo* invented, such as Unilever or Amgen, and cannot be found in any dictionary, or slang, dialect, or arbitrary in the sense that they use common words in a way that is not expected.

From the business perspective there is a strong temptation to select a trademark that is descriptive for the simple reason that it immediately provides the customer with information about the product. However, the downside to a descriptive mark is that the terms are normally used on a wide variety of goods.

Trademarks are only protectable if they have distinctive power, i.e. are capable of distinguishing the goods or services of one owner from those of another, i.e. the origin.

There are some signs that cannot be protected.

- *Names and portraits.* Protection is not possible for the use of a name, portrait, or signature of a living person without his/her approval.
- *Functional marks.* Non-traditional marks such as colors and product designs are not protectable if they are, on the whole, functional. For example, the color yellow has been found to be functional for safety products.
- *Immoral marks.* Marks that refer to e.g. torture, racism, etc.
- *Likelihood of confusion.* The proposed mark is identical to or can cause confusion with an existing trademark.

In most cases the process for selecting a trademark is not simple, but such a process must be in place. The basic steps of a typical selection process are presented in Figure 4.4.

Registering the mark

The law considers a trademark to be a form of (intangible) property. Proprietary rights in relation to a trademark may be established through actual use in the marketplace (^{TM} or ^{SM}), or through registration of the mark (®) with the trademark office (or "trademark registry") in a specific jurisdiction. In some jurisdictions trademark rights can be established via public use, but other countries do not recognize rights arising through use. If trademark owners do not hold registrations for their marks in such jurisdictions, the extent to which they will be able to enforce their rights through trademark infringement proceedings will

Figure 4.4 **Process for developing a trademark**

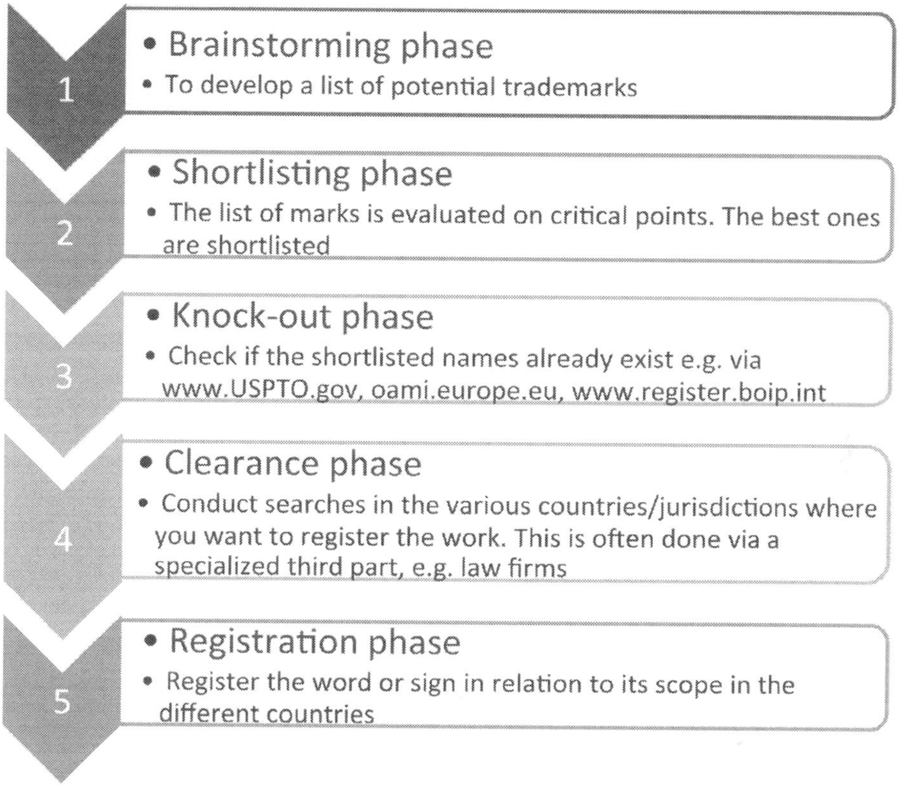

therefore be limited. In cases of dispute, this discrepancy in rights is often referred to as "first to file" as opposed to "first to use".

In the United States and most other countries, unregistered trademarks and names enjoy common law protection. This means a party who adopts and uses a mark in a particular geographic territory is entitled to protection against subsequent use that adopts the same or a similar mark in that same context in the same territory. "Territory" is a relatively unclear and narrow concept that depends on the nature and extent of the use of the mark in a territory.

Let us look again at our example of pipettes. If we run a search on the USPTO database (www.uspto.gov), we find 38 trademarks related to pipettes. Some examples are presented in Figure 4.5.

The requirements for filing a US trademark application are relatively straightforward. Online applications via the USPTO website are possible. For an applicant to receive a filing date, s/he must include:

Figure 4.5 Examples of US registered trade names related to "pipette"

Trade Mark #: 85610923 Apricot Designs Inc. (25/12/2012)	Trade Mark #: 79018385 Precision Pipette Inc. (12/3/2002)	Trade Mark #: 79018385 Gilson Inc. (14/10/2012)

- the required filing fee for at least one class from the US "Acceptable Identification of Goods and Services" list – which is much more extensive and detailed in comparison to the listing used in the European Union
- the name of the applicant
- the name and address of the applicant or attorney for communication
- a clear name or drawing of the mark to be registered
- the identification of the goods and/or services that the mark will be used with (using the "Acceptable Identification of Goods and Services" codes).

A more difficult part of the process is preparing the identification of goods and/or services for which the trademark will be used. The goal is to draft the list of goods and services as broadly as possible because the identification cannot be expanded later on. The USPTO website has an online searchable ID manual that contains the listing of acceptable identifications of goods and services.

In the European Union and most other countries the registration process is fairly similar. A trademark can be registered through a member state(s), e.g. the Benelux Office for Intellectual Property (BOIP – www.boip.int). Registration of one trademark for three classes costs €240, and the trademark protection can later be expanded to other EU member states and other countries in the world using the Madrid Protocol (see below). In the European Union one can also opt to file an EU trademark via the OHIM (https://oami.europa.eu/ohimportal/en/), with a basic fee of €900 for up to three classes and €150 for each additional class. In the European Union the Nice Classification is used, which divides goods and services into 45 categories (or classes). The TMClass tool on the OHIM website makes it easy to find the class and number for which you pursue trademark protection.

There is an important difference between applying for a trademark in the United States and applying in the European Union (and most other countries). In the European Union registration occurs prior to any opposition proceeding, i.e. once an application is reviewed by an examiner and found to be eligible for registration, a registration certificate is issued subject to the mark being open to opposition for a period of typically six months from the date of registration.

Every trademark owner may oppose a registration if the sign is identical to an earlier trademark and filed for identical classes of goods and services. A trademark owner may also oppose a registration of a sign similar to its mark and filed for similar goods and services if the owner can demonstrate there is a likelihood of confusion on the part of the public in the territory in which the earlier trademark is protected.

Figure 4.6 shows some examples of decisions taken by the Board of Appeal of the OHIM (Trade Marks and Designs) in opposition proceedings where it had to assess the existence of a likelihood of confusion between two signs.

A registered trademark represents a set of exclusive rights held by the registered owner, including the right to use the mark in relation to the products or services for which it has been registered. The law in most countries also allows the owner of a registered trademark to prevent unauthorized use of the mark in relation to products or services which are identical or "confusingly" similar to the "registered" products or services, and sometimes even to prevent use in relation to entirely dissimilar products or services.

A peculiar example was Louis Vuitton prohibiting the artist Nadia Plesner from using a Louis Vuitton handbag held by an African child in a painting. Plesner did so nevertheless, and had to pay, by ruling of the court, €5,000 per day when the painting was publicly displayed.[1] Later, during opposition, the court ruled in favour of Ms Plesner based on arguments of, for instance, artistic freedom.

A trademark owner may during the registration procedure oppose a trademark registration. After a mark has been registered the owner of an older trademark may act against the use of the new trademark under certain circumstances.

Once trademark rights are established in a particular jurisdiction, these rights are generally only enforceable in that jurisdiction – a situation which is sometimes referred to as territoriality. However, a range of international trademark laws and systems facilitate the protection of trademarks in more than one country. There are also systems to facilitate the filing, registration, or enforcement of trademark rights in more than one jurisdiction on a regional or global basis. Nevertheless, it is currently

Figure 4.6 Examples of decisions by the OHIM

CASE	CONTESTED	EARLIER	CONFUSINGLY SIMILAR
Biorem vs. Biorema [18]	**BIOREMA** (classes 5, 30, 31, 32)	**BIOREM** (classes 5, 10, 35)	V
Bionorica vs. Bionica [19]	Bionorica (classes 5, 30)	BIONICA (classes 5, 30)	V
Femivia vs. Femibion [20]	**FEMIVIA** (class 5)	femibion (classes 5, 29, 30)	V
Digna BioTech vs. Dignicare [21]	**DIGNA BIOTECH** (classes 1, 5, 9, 10, 16, 35, 38, 40, 41, 42, 44)	**DIGNICARE** (class 10)	X
Biobé vs. Bebe [22]	biobé (classes 20, 25, 35)	bebe bebe Young Care (classes 3, 16, 18, 20, 21, 44)	X
Metabiomax vs. Biomax [23]	**METABIOMAX** (classes 5, 16, 30)	**BIOMAX** (classes 5, 30, 32)	V & X *

* Likelihood of confusion for the goods which are similar, no likelihood of confusion for the goods which have been found dissimilar.

Sources:

Decision of 25 May 2012 – R 100/2011-4 – Biorema/Biorem, http://oami.europa.eu/LegalDocs/BoA/2011/en/R0100_2011-4.pdf;

Decision of 22 May 2013 – R 643/2012-2 – Bionorica/BIONICA (fig. mark), http://oami.europa.eu/LegalDocs/BoA/2012/en/R0643_2012-2.pdf;

Decision of 15 April 2013 – R1021/2012-4 – FEMIVIA/FEMIBION et al., http://oami.europa.eu/LegalDocs/BoA/2012/en/R1021_2012-4.pdf;

Decision of 25 April 2012 – R 422/2011-2 – Dignicare/Digna Biotech (fig. mark), http://oami.europa.eu/LegalDocs/BoA/2011/en/R0422_2011-2.pdf;

Decision of 29 February 2012 – R 2148/2010-2 – biobé (fig. mark)/bebe et al., http://oami.europa.eu/LegalDocs/BoA/2010/en/R2148_2010-2.pdf;

Decision of 30 October 2012 – R2089/2011-2 – Metabiomax/Biomax, http://oami.europa.eu/LegalDocs/BoA/2011/en/R2089_2011-2.pdf.

not possible to file and obtain a single trademark registration that will automatically apply around the world.

The major international system for "facilitating" the registration of trademarks in multiple jurisdictions is commonly known as the Madrid Protocol. This is a centrally administered system for securing trademark registrations in member jurisdictions by extending the protection of an "international registration" obtained through WIPO. This international registration is in turn based upon an application or registration obtained by a trademark applicant in its home jurisdiction. More details can be found at www.wipo.int/madrid/en, where you can also find an overview of the fees related to registration and a fee calculator.

The primary advantage of the Madrid system is that it allows an owner to obtain trademark protection in many jurisdictions by filing one application in one jurisdiction with one set of fees, and make any changes (e.g. changes of name or address) and renew registration across all applicable jurisdictions through a single administrative process. Furthermore, the "coverage" of the international registration may be extended to additional member jurisdictions at any time.

The Madrid Protocol offers cost savings and increased efficiency for trademark holders. The International Trademark Association (undated) summarizes the benefits of the Madrid Protocol as follows:

- one application
- in one place
- with one set of documents
- in one language
- with one fee
- resulting in one registration
- with one number
- one renewal date
- covering more than one country.

Maintaining rights and protections

Trademark rights can be a company's most valuable assets. Like any asset, they need to be protected and maintained.

These rights will cease if a mark is not actively used for a period of time, normally five years in most countries. Failure to use the mark actively in the lawful course of trade may result in its nullity, making it impossible to enforce the trademark against an (alleged) infringer on the grounds of "non-use". It is not necessary for a trademark owner to take enforcement action against all infringement if it can be shown that the owner perceived the infringement to be minor and inconsequential. This is designed to prevent owners from continuously being involved with litigation for fear of cancellation. An owner can at any time commence action for infringement against a third party as long as it had not previously notified this party of its discontent following third-party use and then failed to take action within a reasonable period of time.

If a trademark has not been registered, some countries (especially common law countries) offer protection for the business reputation or goodwill related to unregistered marks, e.g. when a business has been trading under an unregistered trademark for many years, and a rival business starts using the same or a similar mark.

A trademark owner can license the trademark to a third party. However, the owner must reserve the power to exercise quality control over the nature and quantity of the goods and services in a license. If the trademark owner fails to exercise such quality control, the license is considered "naked" and the mark may be abandoned.

A trademark may only be assigned to another party with the goodwill of the business by which the mark is used. Failure to meet this requirement can result in the trademark becoming void.

There are many examples where once-valuable trademarks have become generic, i.e. the trademarks have ceased to function as an indicator of origin and have become the name of a particular type of product. These terms are now generic and available for use by all. If an owner wishes to avoid this, it is essential that all those associated with a trademark understand the requirements. The following guidelines can help protect the value of a trademark.

- *Do not trademark the name of your product.* The trademark may become generic when referring to your brand.
- *When using a trademark in a sentence, always use it as an adjective.* Otherwise, the public may come to see the trademark as the generic name of the product or service. This happened to former trademarks such as bakelite, cellophane, kerosene, biro, thermos...
- *In a sentence, the trademark should be set apart from the normal text in some fashion*, e.g. color, italics, capitals, bold...
- *Monitor the use of your mark.* If the same or a similar trademark is used by more than one company on the same or related goods, the mark may cease to be an indicator of origin.

- *Take legal action when needed.* A publisher should be notified immediately. Likewise, if you see your mark appear in lower-case letters, this is a danger sign.
- *Be consistent in the use of your mark.*
- *Use the appropriate trademark designation:* ® SM TM
- *Develop a trademark usage protocol (SOP).* All companies should have a manual to advise employees and others on the proper use of the company's trademarks.
- *Non-use.* Three to five years of non-use results in a presumption of abandonment.

It is very important to maintain and protect your trademarks. If business goes well, trademarks can represent high economic value. Every year Interbrand determines and ranks the worldwide top brands: Table 4.2 shows the top 20 brands of 2012, together with the value they represent.

Protected geographical status in the European Union

As mentioned in Chapter 1, some industries have specific additional systems related to intellectual property. A typical example is PGS in the European Union for the names of regional foods (European Commission, 2007). Products eligible for PGS are cheeses, meat and meat-based products, fish and seafood-related products, oils and fats, table olives, fruits, vegetables and cereals, bread, pastry and other baker's wares, beer, and other drinks.

The EU rules governing the production of wine (Council Regulation (EC) 1493/1999 on the common organization of the market in wine) are significantly more extensive than the Community trademark law. For spirits there are additional laws (Council Regulation (EC) 1576/89 laying down general rules on the definition, description, and presentation of spirit drinks), providing a double system of protection. The protection of geographical indicators for wines and spirits was the first to be developed on national and EC levels. It is also the only protection which is recognized by TRIPS.

Such protection is closely related to trademarks, but nevertheless different. The legal framework has three specific regimes, as presented in Figure 4.7.

Table 4.2 Top 20 brands in 2012

Rank	Brand	Value (US$ billion)
1	Coca-Cola	77.84
2	Apple	76.57
3	IBM	75.53
4	Google	69.73
5	Microsoft	57.85
6	General Electric	43.68
7	McDonald's	40.06
8	Intel	39.39
9	Samsung	32.89
10	Toyota	30.28
11	Mercedes-Benz	30.10
12	BMW	29.05
13	Disney	27.44
14	Cisco	27.20
15	HP	26.09
16	Gillette	24.90
17	Louis Vuitton	23.58
18	Oracle	22.13
19	Nokia	21.01
20	Amazon	18.63

Source: Interbrand (2012).

More information on the registration of products as a form of PGS can be found at ec.europa.eu/agriculture/quality/index_en.htm, which also gives a complete list of PGS-registered products.

In 2008 there were approximately 820 products listed in the European Register of PDO and PGI, including beer, but wine and spirits excluded (European Commission, 2010). The turnover of these products increased between 2005 and 2007, reaching €14.2 billion (Figure 4.8). Approximately 30 percent is exported outside the European Union.

The legislation came into force in 1992 and was updated in March 2006 (Council Regulation (EC) 509/2006 on agricultural products and foodstuffs as traditional specialities guaranteed; Council Regulation (EC) 510/2006 on the protection of geographical indications and designations

Figure 4.7 The three regimes of PGS

Protected designation of origin (PDO)

The name of an area, place, or exceptionally a country used as a designation for an agricultural product or foodstuff:

- which comes from this region
- whose quality and characteristics are specifically related to this region
- whose processing or production takes place in this region.

Example: Camembert de Normandie from France

Protected geographical indication (PGI)

The name of an area, place, or exceptionally a country used as a description of an agricultural product or foodstuff:

- which comes from this region
- which has specific quality, goodwill, or characteristics related to this geographical region
- whose processing or production takes place within the region.

Example: Scottish beef from the UK (Scotland)

Traditional speciality guaranteed (TSG)

This is a trademark for an agricultural product or foodstuff which has a specific set of features, different from other, similar products. It needs to be manufactured using traditional ingredients or processed and produced in a traditional way.

Example: Gueuze Lambic, a Belgian traditional beer

of origin for agricultural products and foodstuffs). In principle, similar protection to a PGI could be obtained through a collective trademark. However, indications which serve exclusively to identify the place of origin of goods are not registerable as trademarks (Council Regulation (EC) 207/2009 of 26 February 2009 on the Community trademark, Article 7; Directive 2008/95/EC of the European Parliament and Council of 22 October 2008 to approximate the laws of member states relating to trademarks, Article 3).

Trademarks that have been registered before the registration of a PDO or PGI may continue to be used. The registration of an equivalent trademark after PDO or PGI came in place is not allowed. There is no protection for these names outside the European Union. Nevertheless, the European Union has signed a number of bilateral agreements, for example with Canada, Australia, Chile, Colombia, Mexico, and South

Figure 4.8 **Contribution of different PDO/PGI products to total turnover, 2007**

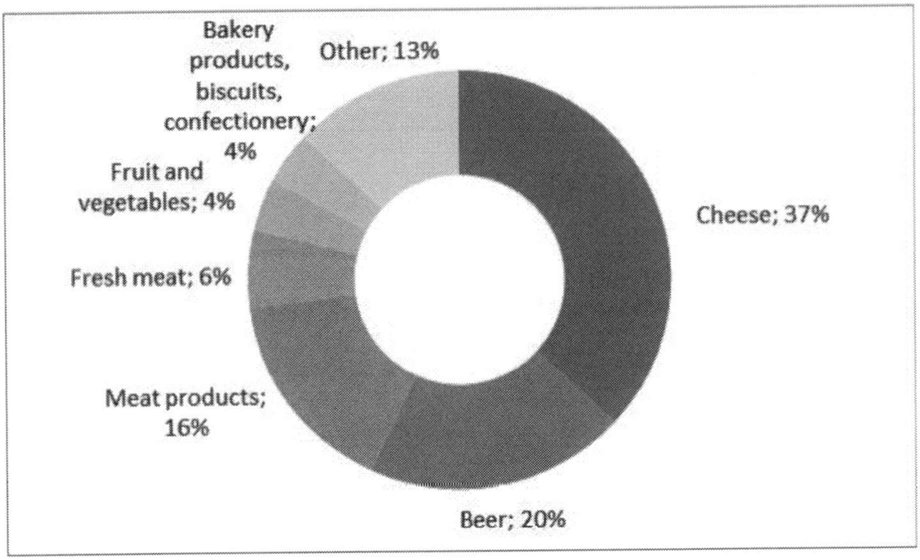

Source: European Commission (2010).

Africa. No agreement exists with the United States, where many names that are protected in the European Union are often commonly used generic terms, such as Parmesan cheese. Hence in the United States it is possible to buy a bottle of champagne which is produced in the United States. Nevertheless, there is some degree of protection for US regional designation under the certification mark law, e.g. the registered trademark "Grown in Idaho" for potatoes.

Domain names

Domain names are essential for the promotion of corporate identity and product awareness in the modern era. They should be regarded like any other valuable corporate assets.

The advent of the domain name system has led to attempts by trademark holders to enforce their rights over domain names that are similar or identical to their existing trademarks, particularly by seeking control over the domain names at issue. As with dilution protection, enforcing trademark rights over domain name owners involves protecting a trademark outside the obvious context of its consumer market, because domain names are global and not limited by goods or services. This conflict is more easily resolved when the domain name user actually used its website to compete with the trademark owner.

There are various forms of domain name/trademark abuse.

- *Cybersquatting:* an unlicensed user registering the trademark as a domain name to pressure a payment (or other benefit) from the lawful mark owner.
- *Typo squatters:* registering common spelling mistakes of trademarks as domain.
- *"Gripe-site":* a type of site devoted to critique or mockery of a person, company, or subject, e.g. using a registered trademark in a domain such as "[trademark]sucks.com".

There are also disputes arising from subdomains, when a third party uses a protected mark in a web address such as "[trademark].[legitimatedomain].com".

This clash of the new technology with pre-existing trademark rights has resulted in several high-profile decisions as the courts of many countries tried to address the issue coherently (and not always successfully) within the framework of existing trademark law. As a website itself was not the product being purchased, there was no actual consumer confusion, and so initial interest confusion was a concept applied instead. Initial interest confusion is defined as customer confusion that creates an initial interest in a competitor's "product" (in the online context, another party's website). Even though initial interest confusion is dispelled by the time any actual sale occurs, it allows a trademark infringer to capitalize on the goodwill associated with the original mark.

Domain names consist of a number of domain levels. For example, in a two-level domain name such as food2know.org, the portion of the name to the right side (i.e. ".org") is the top-level domain (TLD), and the portion of the name to the left (i.e. "food2know") is the second-level domain (SLD). Many internet users also recognize the three-letter string "www" preceding the domain name. This portion of the domain is typically considered a "subdomain" which is selected by the host computer.

The SLD is usually selected by the website owner, and is typically used as a source identifier in the domain name. The SLD can consist of a trademark or service mark. The most common TLDs are termed global or generic TLDs (gTLDs). Some commonly known gTLDs are listed below:

- *.eu* – organizations in the European Union (e.g. www.bujinkan.eu)
- *.com* – commercial enterprises
- *.net* – networks
- *.org* – non-profit organizations (e.g. www.food2know.org)
- *.biz* – businesses
- *.edu* – educational institutions
- *.gov* – US government entities
- *.be* – Belgian websites (e.g. www.ugent.be)
- *.mil* – US military
- *.int* – international organizations.

The international legal development has also led to the creation of the Uniform Domain Name Dispute Resolution Policy (UDPR) from the Internet Corporation for Assigned Names and Numbers (ICANN) and other dispute policies for specific countries (such as the CEPINA-DNS procedure in Belgium, and Nominet UK's dispute resolution system) which attempt to streamline the process of resolving who should own a domain name (without dealing with other infringement issues such as damages). This is particularly desirable to trademark owners when the domain name registrant may be in another country, or even anonymous.

The goal of the UDPR is to create a lower-cost administrative process for the resolution of domain name disputes. In a UDRP proceeding, the trademark owner must prove three elements:

- that the domain name at issue is identical or confusingly similar to a trademark in which the owner of the trademark has rights
- that the domain name registrant has no rights to or legitimate interest with respect to the domain name
- that the domain name has been registered *and* is being used in a bad faith.

While a UDRP proceeding is beneficial in that it can result in a speedy and lower-cost disposition of a domain dispute, the only available remedies in such a proceeding are the cancellation or transfer of the disputed domain name.

To secure a domain name, it must first be registered with an ICANN-accredited registrar responsible for the global coordination of the internet's system of unique identifiers, including domain names. There are over 150 registrars accredited by ICANN (see icann.org/registrars/accredited-list.html). Accredited registrars and domain name holders must implement and follow the UDPR. Domain names are typically granted by registrars on a first-come-first-served basis. Registering a domain name with a registrar does not grant trademark protection for the domain.

To address cybersquatting, the United States enacted the Anticybersquatting Consumer Protection Act (ACPA). The ACPA identifies cybersquatting as follows:

- A person shall be liable in a civil action by the owner of a mark, including a personal name which is protected as a mark under this section, if, without regard to the goods or services of the parties, that person:
  - has a bad faith intent to profit from that mark, including a personal name which is protected as a mark under this section and
  - registers, is trading in, or uses a domain name that is identical or confusingly similar to that mark, uses a famous mark, etc., at the time of registration of the domain name.

Thus in order for a trademark owner to bring a claim under the ACPA, the owner must establish that:

- the mark is distinctive or famous
- the domain name registrant acted in a bad faith by use of the mark
- the domain name and the trademark are either identical or confusingly similar.

To register an .eu domain name, the average price in 2007 was €30. If you wish to recover a name from someone who is misusing your name (or trade name), you must first register your case at ADR (Alternative Dispute Resolution) from EurID, which costs between €1,850 and €3,710. After adding the costs of lawyers, one easily spends €3,000–6,000. For this amount one can register five domain names preventively for a minimum of 20 years.

For instance, we looked at the trademark Food2Know earlier. After registering the name and logo, the following domain names were also registered:

- www.food2know.be
- www.food2know.com
- www.food2know.org.

Preferably, it would be good to register the .eu domain name as well, since this currently gives a high relevance score in search engines such as Google.

Notes

1. Civil Rights Court, 's Gravenhage, Holland, ruling No. KG RK 10-214, 27 January 2011.

Copyrights

Abstract: Copyright is another important form of intellectual property. It is not just restricted to artists, novelists, musicians, etc. – scientists and technologists can also make good use of this type of IP. This chapter explains in more depth what copyright protection is and describes the legislation covering it. Software can be considered as specific form of copyright, illustrated in a case study of PredOxyPack.

Key words: copyright, definition, legislation, registration, software.

Defining copyright

Copyright (Figure 5.1) is an exclusive right granted to the author or creator by the law of a country for his or her original work, including the right to copy, distribute, and adapt the work. Exceptions and limitations to these rights strive to balance the public interest in the wide distribution of the material produced and encouraging creativity. Exceptions include fair dealing and fair use. This type of use does not require the permission of the copyright owner; all other uses require the owner's permission. Owners can license or permanently transfer their exclusive rights to others.

Copyright is, literally, the right to copy, though in legal terms "the right to control copying" is more accurate. You can buy a book, read it, color it, throw it away, but you cannot copy it, publish it on the internet, etc. Copyrights are exclusive statutory rights to exercise control over copying and other exploitation of the works for a specific period of time. The copyright owner therefore has:

Figure 5.1 Copyright, another form of protecting your IP

- an exclusive, positive right to copy and exploit the copyrighted work, or license others to do so
- a negative right to prevent anyone else from copying or exploiting the work without consent, with the possibility of legal penalties if they do so.

Copyright does not protect ideas, only their specific expression or fixation in a tangible form. In most countries, copyright arises upon creation or fixation and does not need to be registered. Copyright protection applies for a specific period of time, after which the work is said to enter the public domain. This term start at the creation of the original work and runs for minimum 50 years after the death of the author. To be protectable, it is not required that the work is artistic, esthetic, or beautiful. The only criterion is that the work is original in the sense that it is the author's own intellectual creation.

An original sculpture is copyrightable whether it is made of wood, stone, bronze, chocolate, butter, or ice. In the case of the edible media, there can be a "fixation" issue. If a chocolate-based sculpture is created and afterwards eaten, it is temporal and not fixed. This problem can be solved by the creator taking a photograph or making a mold to satisfy the Copyright Act's fixation requirement: even if the original is destroyed or eaten, the intangible copyright endures to the extent the work has been preserved in some form from which it can be reproduced.

Original authorship is often embodied in advertising and marketing materials and packaging. The primary issues of concern in these areas are copyright ownership, avoiding infringement, and preserving legal actions through registration. In the US registration is mainly done so a copyright owner can preserve its ability to claim statutory damages – remedies that are not available if infringement commences before registration. The registration process also compels an examination of authorship/ownership issues as well as necessitating a review of whether any pre-existing material is embodied in a work, which may give rise to a need to obtain permission for the use of such material.

In European countries registration is mainly done to obtain some kind objective evidence. By registering, the author can prove s/he has made the work and the date on which s/he made it. This can help to provide the necessary proof in an infringement case.

In many instances a business may develop recipes related to food products. To the extent such works contain original expression, copyright law protects them, with the caveat that the underlying methods and procedures are not protected by copyright. In the United States this also applies for software. Software with methods therein may be protectable and enforceable, provided that duplication can be proven. In the European Union software is protected under a *lex specialis*. The source code and all preparatory works are protected as a computer program. A computer program is assimilated with a work of literature and therefore protected under the specific regime of software copyright.

For software, owners often want to ensure secrecy, and copyright allows this. When an owner needs secrecy of works such as recipes and software source code, it can register the work by providing sufficient identifying material instead of the normally required copy of the work. The identifying material may have confidential portions redacted to preserve secrecy.

Three simple rules control the initial ownership of copyright.

- Ownership of copyright vests initially in the author or authors (a natural person, not an enterprise) of the work, i.e. a person who creates an original work automatically becomes the copyright owner.

- When a work is made for hire, the employer or commissioning party needs to obtain the rights from the author by a written agreement. The exception is in cases of software, when the employer or commissioning party is deemed to be the author. In the United States, however, when a work is made for hire, the employer or commissioning party is deemed to be the author.
- When there is more than one author, the authors of a joint work are co-owners of copyright in the work.

Although these rules are relatively simple, determining authorship can be difficult.

In the United States, when authors cannot agree on authorship the Copyright Office will register conflicting claims to copyright in the same work. To avoid such a dispute, it is always best to try to resolve authorship/ownership issues at an early stage. For an employer, employment contracts should be used to define scope of employment and any work being done by independent contractors, e.g. advertising companies should be covered by an agreement that assigns any copyrights.

In the United States employers do not need to have an agreement with their employees to create a work under the definition of work made for hire. Employment contracts, however, are often useful in settling questions involving whether a particular work was prepared in the "scope of employment". Clear policies often avoid problems in this respect. On the other hand, the law requires specially ordered and commissioned works to be identified in writing as "work for hire". In addition, even if there is a written agreement as to "work for hire" status, only the specifically enumerated types of works are eligible to be considered "work for hire".

In the United States the authors of a joint work may be natural persons or other entities by virtue of "works for hire", or a combination of both where some contributions are "work for hire" and other contributions are not. In the case of multiple employees creating a work for the same employer, there is only one author, the employer, so that such a creation is not a joint work. For works that are jointly owned, unless there is an agreement to the contrary, any joint owner is free to exploit the copyright in the entire work. The other joint owners, however, have a right to share the profits made from the exploitation of the work.

In the European Union there is no full harmonization of copyright legislation between the different member states. Some directives touch on certain aspects of copyrights, but the issue of ownership and co-authorship has not yet been harmonized – the legislation of the member state where protection is sought will provide answers to questions of ownership and co-authorship. With regard to copyright on computer programs, the Software Directive states that when a program is created by an employee in the execution of his/her duties or following the instructions given by an employer, the employer exclusively shall be entitled to exercise all economic rights in the program so created, unless otherwise provided by the contract.

Copyright and legislation

The first copyright statute was the British Statute of Anne of 1710, the full title of which was "An Act for the Encouragement of Learning, by vesting the Copies of Printed Books in the Authors or purchasers of such Copies, during the Times therein mentioned" (Figure 5.2).

The copyright concept emerged in eighteenth-century Europe in relation to printed new books and related authorship. During the European Renaissance and Neoclassical periods the writer was regarded as an instrument, not an independent creator, and was seen as using external sources to create a work of inspiration. In the eighteenth century the view on the source of inspiration within the writer changed, in such a way that special talents and giftedness were considered the basis for creating works of inspiration and uniqueness. The concept of authors as original creators and owners of their work emerged partly from the new concept of property rights and John Locke's theory that individuals were "owners of themselves". In Locke's view, individuals invested their labor in natural goods, and so created property (Hart, 2012; Tuckness, 2012). Authors were argued to be the owners of their work because they had invested their labor in creating it. Nevertheless, confusion has remained about the nature of copyright ever since the *Donaldson v. Becket* case, which was heard in 1774 by Britain's House of Lords, about whether copyright is the natural law right of the author or the statutory grant of a limited monopoly (Rose, 1988). One theory holds that copyright's origin occurs at the creation of a work, and another that its origin exists only through the copyright statute.

Copyright laws are partially standardized through international and regional agreements such as the Berne Convention and the European copyright directives. The Berne Convention was first established in 1886, and subsequently renegotiated in 1896 (Paris), 1908 (Berlin),

Figure 5.2 The British Statute of Anne, dated 1710

(261) Cap 19

Anno Octavo

Annæ Reginæ.

An Act for the Encouragement of Learning, by Vesting the Copies of Printed Books in the Authors or Purchasers of such Copies, during the Times therein mentioned.

Whereas Printers, Booksellers, and other Persons have of late frequently taken the Liberty of Printing, Reprinting, and Publishing, or causing to be Printed, Reprinted, and Published Books, and other Writings, without the Consent of the Authors or Proprietors of such Books and Writings, to their very great Detriment, and too often to the Ruin of them and their Families: For Preventing therefore such Practices for the future, and for the Encouragement of Learned Men to Compose and Write useful Books; May it please Your Majesty, that it may be Enacted, and be it Enacted by the Queens most Excellent Majesty, by and with the Advice and Consent of the Lords Spiritual and Temporal, and Commons in this present Parliament Assembled, and by the Authority of the same, That from and after the Tenth Day of April, One thousand seven hundred and ten, the Author of any Book or Books already Printed, who hath not Transferred to any other the Copy or Copies of such Book or Books, Share or Shares thereof, or the Bookseller or Booksellers, Printer or Printers, or other Person or Persons, who hath or have Purchased or Acquired the Copy or Copies of any Book or Books, in order to Print or Reprint the same, shall have the sole Right and Liberty of Printing such Book and Books for the Term of One and twenty Years, to Commence from the said Tenth Day of April, and no longer; and that the Author of any Book or Books already Composed and not Printed and Published, or that shall hereafter be Composed, and his Assignee, or Assigns, shall have the sole Liberty of Printing and Reprinting such Book and Books for the Term of fourteen

Ttt 2 teen

1928 (Rome), 1948 (Brussels), 1967 (Stockholm), and 1971 (Paris). The convention relates to literary and artistic works, which include films, and requires its member states to provide protection for every production in the literary, scientific, and artistic domain. The Berne Convention has a number of core features, including the principle of national treatment, which holds that each state party to the convention will give citizens of other member states the same rights of copyright that it gives its own citizens.

Another core feature is the establishment of minimum standards of national copyright legislation, in that each member state agrees to certain basic rules which its national laws must contain, though member states can if they wish increase the amount of protection given to copyright owners. One important rule is that the term of copyright is to be a minimum of the author's lifetime plus 50 years. This can vary in different countries, e.g. in the European Union it is plus 70 years. In case of multiple authors it is 70 years after the death of the longest-living author/creator. Another important basic rule established by the Berne Convention is that copyright arises with the creation of a work and does not depend upon any formality such as a system of public registration – previously, some countries did require registration of copyright. Nevertheless, registering is still a good thing to do to establish an "official date" for your creation.

The Berne Convention also enshrined limitations and exceptions to copyright, enabling the reproduction of literary and artistic works without the copyright owners' prior permission. The detail of these exceptions was left to national copyright legislation. The so-called three-step test holds that an exception is only permitted "in certain special cases, provided that such reproduction does not conflict with a normal exploitation of the work and does not unreasonably prejudice the legitimate interests of the author". Free use of copyrighted work is expressly permitted in the case of quotations from lawfully published works, illustration for teaching purposes, and news reporting.

In the 1980s the European Community started to regard copyright as an element in the creation of a single market. Since 1991 the European Union has passed a number of directives on the subject, designed to harmonize copyright laws in member states in certain key areas, such as computer programs, databases, and the internet. The directives aimed to reduce obstacles to the free movement of goods and services within the European Union, such as for example in rental rights, satellite broadcasting, copyright term, and resale rights.

Important developments in copyright at the international level in the 1990s include the 1994 TRIPS agreement. TRIPS was negotiated at the end of the Uruguay Round of the General Agreement on Tariffs and Trade (GATT), and contains a number of provisions on copyright. Compliance with TRIPS is required of countries wishing to be members of the WTO. Member states must comply with the Berne Convention and all its provisions, except for the provision on moral rights. They need to bring computer programs and databases within the scope of works covered by copyright law, and to provide for rental rights in at least computer programs and films. Where copyright term (duration of copyright) is calculated other than by reference to the life of a natural person, states must give a minimum term of 50 years calculated from either the date of authorized publication or the creation of the work.

The Anti-Counterfeiting Trade Agreement (ACTA) is a proposed plurilateral treaty which is claimed by its proponents to respond "to the increase in global trade of counterfeit goods and pirated copyright protected works" (European Commission, 2012). The scope of ACTA is broad, including counterfeit physical goods as well as "internet distribution and information technology".

In October 2007 the United States, the European Community, Switzerland, and Japan announced that they would negotiate ACTA. Other countries have joined the negotiations: Australia, the Republic of Korea, New Zealand, Mexico, Jordan, Morocco, Singapore, the United Arab Emirates, and Canada. The ACTA negotiations have been largely conducted in secrecy, with very little information being officially disclosed. However, on 22 May 2008 a discussion paper about the proposed agreement was uploaded to Wikileaks, and newspaper reports about the secret negotiations quickly followed (Wikileaks, 2008).

Obtaining copyright

In principle, the first author/creator of any new material gets the copyright. This always has to be a natural person(s), not a legal entity. An enterprise can acquire the rights to copyright for commercialization purposes via transfer. This must be done explicitly and in writing, e.g. via a contract. New-crafted, copyright-protected material can include a copyright notice, although this is not legally required. Thus the absence of such a notice does not mean that one can copy without permission the original, copyright-protected material.

A few simple steps can be followed to add a copyright notice.

- Add the symbol © or the word "Copyright", or both.
- Mention the first date when the material was created, or the period when the work started and was elaborated on.
- Mention the name of the author.
- Mention the rights the author allows, e.g. "all rights reserved", meaning the author obtains all possible rights.

It is also possible to add more extensive disclaimers regarding copyright to one's work, e.g. the one on the beginning of this book.

Copyright law is different from country to country, and in about 20 states a copyright notice is required for a work to be protected. Before 1989 all published works in the United States had to contain a copyright notice – the © symbol followed by the publication date and copyright owner's name – to be protected by copyright. This is no longer the case and a copyright notice is now optional in the United States, though they are still used. The same often applies in other countries, e.g. the Berne Convention in the European Union.

In all countries that are members of the Berne Convention, copyright is automatic and need not be obtained through official registration with any government office. Once an idea has been expressed or reduced to tangible form, for example by securing it in a fixed medium (such as a drawing, sheet music, photograph, a videotape, or a computer file), the copyright holder is entitled to enforce his or her exclusive rights. However, while registration is not needed to exercise copyright, in countries where the laws provide for registration, it serves as objective, hard evidence of a valid copyright.

After initial ownership of copyright is established through authorship, copyrights may be transferred. Copyrights can be bought and sold much like other properties. In the individual licensing model the copyright owner authorizes the use of the work against remuneration and under the conditions specified by the license. These conditions may be complex, since the exclusive rights granted by copyright to the copyright owner can be split territorially or with respect to language, the sequence of uses may be fixed, and the number of copies to be made and their subsequent use may also be specified. Furthermore, sublicenses and representation agreements may be included.

Copyright is an important form of protecting IP and can provide quite some income. A nice example is Ms J.K. Rowling, who went from being rather poor to becoming one of the richest women in entertainment. According to *Forbes* (2007), her net worth in 2007 was estimated at US$1 billion. J.K. Rowling might have negotiated royalties in the order of 10 percent, but given her track record she may well be doing significantly better. A good author could expect a 10 percent royalty on net sales. The fifth book in Rowling's Harry Potter series, *Harry Potter and the Order of the Phoenix*, had initial print runs in the order of 13 million copies total, of which 8.5 million were sold in the United States. The US list price is US$29.99, but most sales seem to have been made at around $17. Hence 8.5 million US sales at $17 per book give $144.5 million in net sales. This results in US$14.5 million royalties for Rowling.

Another nice example is the agreement in 2009 between author James Patterson and the Hachette Book Group publisher whereby Patterson would receive $150 million for writing 17 books in 2012. These are two of the more lucrative stories. In general average earnings were $10,000 a year (*The Guardian*, 2011). This amount is significantly skewed by top earners: half the writers earn less than $500.

Of course, copyright is not only possible for novels and music, but also for scientific software, designs, books, etc.

A contract with regard to all or some of the rights in a copyrighted work is known as a copyright license. A copyright assignment is an immediate and irrevocable transfer of the copyright owner's entire interest in all or some of the rights in the copyrighted work. Many jurisdictions have specific legislation in place to protect the author in contractual relations. If these rules are not obeyed, the clause or the entire contract may be found null and void. It is thus recommended to draft copyright agreements precisely, especially when one of the parties is the author of the original work.

Copyright licensing and assignment cover only the specified territory. There are significant differences in national laws with regards to copyright licensing and assignment. Nevertheless, the creator keeps the right to respect regarding the work: he or she can block modification, mutilating changes, use for immoral or unethical purposes, etc.

Copyright licenses, at a minimum, define the copyrighted works and rights subject to the license, the territories or geographic region in which the license applies, its term or length, and the consideration (such as a lump-sum payment or royalties) for the license. Depending on how the work may be used, different licenses need to be acquired. For example, the activity of distributing a book will require a license for the right to print the book and the right to distribute copies to the public. Because sometimes the original format needs to be adapted to fit a specific size of book, it may also be necessary to obtain a license for the right to modify the original work. If the book is to be edited or modified the copyright owner may include control over or approval of the editing process, or of the final result.

Different types of exclusive licenses exist, such as those that exclude the licensor from use of the licensed copyrighted work in the relevant region and for the stated time period. Or exclusive licenses may prevent the licensor from licensing to other parties in the geographic region and during the license term. There are also various types of non-exclusive licenses, where the licensor chooses to offer licenses to third parties and multiple licensees can exercise their rights in a specific territory. If a licensing agreement does not specify that the license is exclusive it may nonetheless be deemed exclusive depending on the language of the contract. Depending on local laws, the owner of an exclusive license may be deemed the "copyright owner" of that work and bring charges for copyright infringement.

The term or length of the copyright license is not allowed to exceed the copyright term specified by local law. Licenses may establish various payment arrangements, such as royalties as a percentage of sales or a stepped percentage of sales, e.g. 5 percent of sales up to 50,000 units and 2.5 percent of sales in excess thereof. The trigger for royalty payments may be sales or other factors. Minimum royalty payments are arrangements whereby a minimum up-front payment is made and then used to offset the percentage on sales. The up-front payment may be non-refundable if sales royalties do not reach the amount of the payment. Minimum royalty arrangements may be accompanied by marketing duties for the licensee, e.g. best effort or reasonable efforts to market and promote the copyrighted work.

Collective rights management is the licensing of copyright and related rights by organizations acting on behalf of rights owners. Collective management organizations, such as collecting societies, typically represent groups of copyright and related rights owners, such as authors, composers, publishers, writers, photographers, musicians, and performers. The following exclusive rights granted under copyright law are commonly collectively managed by collecting societies:

- the right to public performance
- the right to broadcasting
- mechanical reproduction rights for recorded music
- performing rights for dramatic works
- rights of reprographic reproduction of literary and musical works
- related rights, e.g. the rights of performers and producers in recorded music when used in broadcasts.

Some examples of such collecting societies are Güfa in Germany for film producers and SABAM in Belgium for authors and composers. Additional information can be found on the WIPO website.

One of the informational requirements in registering copyright in a work is to identify pre-existing copyrighted material that is present in the copyright application. This is important for registration purposes because copyright in a derivative work is limited to the newly added material; the pre-existing material is protected by its own prior copyright. To the extent that a work "unlawfully" uses pre-existing material, the law may invalidate copyright protection.

Registration

Although copyright comes about spontaneously when something original is created and is covered by relevant legislation, registering/notifying copyright provides an invaluable source of information about copyrighted works. Moreover, for copyright owners the registration process is valuable in examining the issues of copyright ownership and the use of third-party materials. Registration is a simple procedure that can lead to evidence when questions arise on authorship, creation date, and ownership.

There are different ways to register your copyrighted material.

- *Notarial deed.* You can request a notary to draft an authentic deed describing your work. The deed together with all material subject to copyrights is left in the archives of the notary, and this will prove a priority date for the work produced or created. This is of course a rather expensive exercise. The cost depends on the size of the dossier (minimum €500 in Belgium).
- *Registration offices.* Some countries have official registration offices linked to the government. In Belgium, for instance, AHRED (Administratie van het kadaster, de registratie en de domeinen) can provide a priority date on your copyright-related documents. The cost is approximately €30.
- *The bailiff.* You can request a bailiff to make an official note that you possess on a certain date specific material, and take a description of these materials. The cost is approximately €250.
- *Registered letter.* You can send a registered letter to yourself, but make sure you can prove that the letter you claim was in the envelope was indeed in that envelope. This can be done by cutting an opening next

to the stamp so that the date stamp of the post office is clearly marked also on the letter in the envelope, or by folding the letter in such a way that it serves as the envelope. This system is often referred to as "poor man's evidence".

- *Escrow*. For software programs you can deposit all material at a recognized independent service provider, called an escrow agent (e.g. see www.escroweurope.com).
- *Official deposit*. Recently several countries have established government-related offices where one can deposit new ideas and newly created, copyright-protected materials. In the United States this is the US Copyright Office, where electronic deposits can also be made at a cost of approximately US$35. In the Benelux countries this can be done online at the BOIP as an i-depot. A one-time deposit costs €35.

None of these registration methods creates any rights for the depositor. They merely serve as a – valuable – means of proof of date, existence, and authorship.

Possible ways to protect software: case study of PredOxyPack

According to TRIPS Article 10, software as such is protected as literature under the Berne Convention, e.g. by copyright. In Belgium software is protected via an addition to the copyright law.[1] Databases or collections of data which were created by human intervention are also protected under TRIPS.

In Europe, according to the EPC, software as such cannot be patented. Since the 1980s the USPTO has moved more towards patentability of software, and since 2000 the scope of protection is getting broader. Europe did not want to discriminate against EU software producers, and so has allowed software patents since 1987 under EPC Article 52.[2] Nevertheless, for the EPO it is of crucial importance that the software results in a technical effect, e.g. software embedded in a new machine.

Unfortunately, the issue still remains highly uncertain in Europe, resulting in the fact that the United States is far ahead regarding the protection of software by means of a patent.

PredOxyPack

Van Bree et al. (2010) developed a model to predict the oxygen permeability of different polymers used for food packaging. The software used underlying databases also created by the research team. The software was initially run under Matlab® and was available on a CD-ROM. It was not necessary to protect this technology as a patent, although a patent application could be written to provide an official date or an act of registration, i.e. creating prior art. The chance of getting a patent granted in the European Union would be nil, but there would be a (small) chance of getting it granted in the United States. Nevertheless, the software program and related database are both protected under the Berne Convention by copyright.

To get a clear date and registration, a short description of the software and related databases was registered via an i-depot (No. 034778, Figure 5.3) at the BOIP.

Additional hurdles were introduced to protect the intellectual property. First of all a name was created. Initially "Proxypack" was considered, but the domain name Proxypack.com had already been taken. Therefore the first choice was "DiffOxyPack", which was finally changed to "PredOxyPack®". This name is quite strange, being somewhere between suggestive and completely novel.

The name was registered as a trademark in the Benelux countries for the following classes (list of goods and services).

- *Class 1:* Chemicals used in industry, science, and photography, and in agriculture, horticulture, and forestry; unprocessed artificial resins and plastics; manures; fire-extinguishing compositions; tempering and soldering preparations; chemical substances for preserving foodstuffs; tanning substances; adhesives used in industry.
- *Class 17:* Rubber, guttapercha, gum, asbestos, mica, and goods made from these materials and not included in other classes; plastics in extruded form for use in manufacture; packing, stopping, and insulating materials; flexible pipes, not of metal.
- *Class 42:* Scientific and technological services and research and design relating thereto; industrial analysis and research services; design and development of computer hardware and software.

Figure 5.3 The i-depot of PredOxyPack

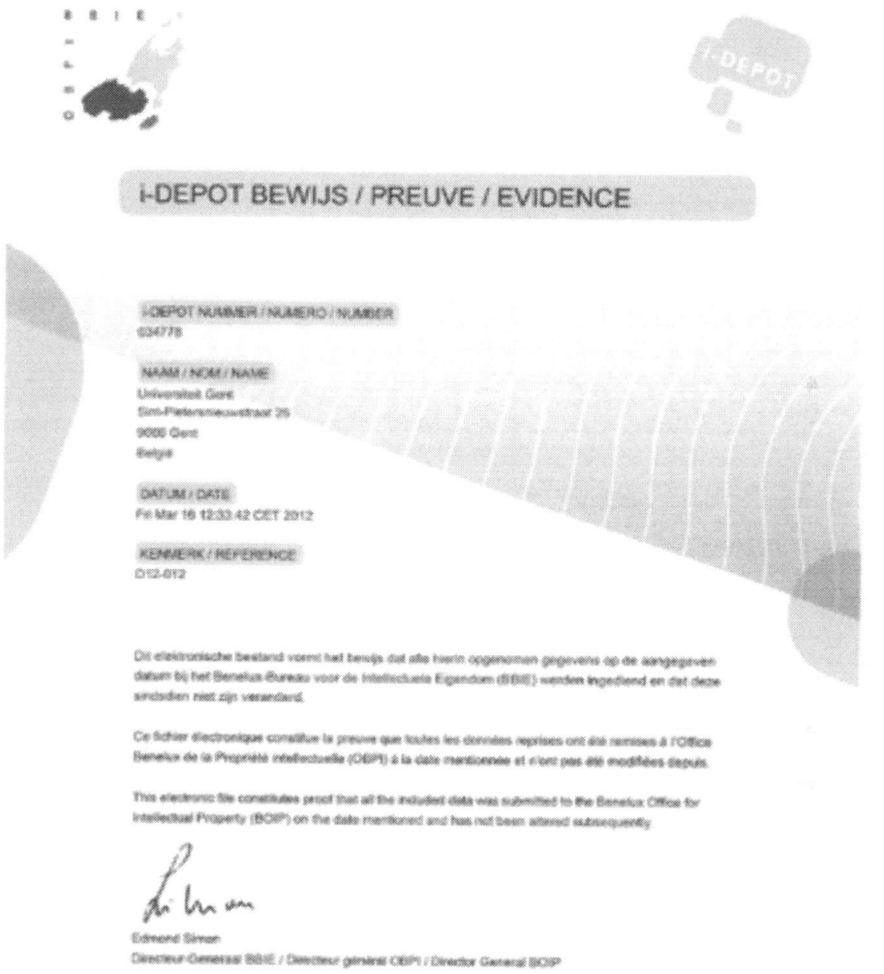

i-DEPOT

i-DEPOT BEWIJS / PREUVE / EVIDENCE

i-DEPOT NUMMER / NUMERO / NUMBER

NAAM / NOM / NAME

DATUM / DATE

Fri Mar 16 12:33:42 CET 2012

KENMERK / REFERENCE

The total cost was €240, and the trademark was granted on 13 October 2011 (Figure 5.4).

Another hurdle was created by protecting artwork and advertising around PredOxyPack (Figure 5.5). A brochure is considered artwork and is covered under copyright law.

Figure 5.4 The registered trade name "PredOxyPack"

BENELUX-BUREAU
VOOR DE
INTELLECTUELE
EIGENDOM

BEWIJS VAN INSCHRIJVING

0908692

1232926 22.09.2011, 08.43

22.09.2021

Universiteit Gent

Coupure links 653

9000 Gent,
België.

PredOxyPack

Kl 01 Chemische producten voor industriële, wetenschappelijke en fotografische doeleinden, alsmede voor land-, tuin- en bosbouwkundige doeleinden; kunstharsen als grondstof, plastics als grondstof; meststoffen; brandblusmiddelen; hardings- en soldeerpreparaten voor metalen; chemische producten voor het conserveren van voedingsmiddelen; looistoffen; kleefstoffen voor industriële doeleinden.

Kl 17 Rubber, guttapercha, gummi, asbest, mica en hieruit vervaardigde producten voor zover niet begrepen in andere klassen; halfbewerkte plastic producten; dichtings-, pakking- en isolatiemateriaal; niet-metalen buigzame buizen.

Kl 42 Wetenschappelijke en technologische diensten, alsmede bijbehorende onderzoeks- en ontwerpdiensten; dienstverlening op het gebied van industriële analyse en industrieel onderzoek; ontwerpen en ontwikkelen van computers en van software.

01 17 42

10/01/2012

10.01.2012

13/10/2011

PredOxyPack

Den Haag, 11 januari 2012

Edmond Simon
Directeur-Generaal

Figure 5.4 The PredOxyPack brochure

To get broad protection regarding the website, various domain names were registered:

- predoxypack.be
- predoxypack.net
- predoxypack.eu
- predoxypack.com
- predopack.eu
- predopack.net
- predopack.com
- predopack.be
- predo2pack.com
- predo2pack.be
- predo2pack.net
- predo2pack.eu
- predoxipack.com
- predoxipack.be
- predoxipack.eu
- predoxipack.net.

This was done via www.gandi.net at a total cost of €229.63 for a period of one year.

Since it is quite easy to copy software on a CD-ROM, it was decided to convert the software to a stand-alone version which would be accessed via the internet and did not require Matlab. An e-shop was set up on the PredOxyPack website (www.predoxypack.be), where users purchase a license to use the simulating software. The IP rights (software, database, trademark, domain names, and copyrights) were transferred from Ghent University to Pack4Food vzw on 20 January 2012 in return for a royalty of 7 percent on net sales for a period of ten years and sales-related stage payments.

The next chapter discusses assessing the value of intellectual property.

Notes

1. "Wet van 30 juni 1994 houdende de omzetting van de richtlijn betreffende de rechtsbescherming van computerprogramma's", *Belgisch Staatsblad*, 27 July 1994.
2. T0026/86.

Assessing the financial value of IP

Abstract: Creating and protecting new IP are a first crucial step in successful commercialization and for building and keeping competitive advantage. For business development, e.g. licensing, it is important to assess the financial value of new IP. This can be done via simple methods using industrial standards or rules of thumb for a specific industrial sector, such as the "25 percent rule" or "FRAND". More labor-intensive methods are based on discounted cash flow (DCF) techniques. Various DCF systems are presented that can take into account the level of uncertainty or the risks associated with a specific project or technology in the future.

Key words: valorization, financial assessment, industrial standards, 25 percent rule, FRAND and DCF methods.

Introduction

Creating and protecting new intellectual property can be fun and add to one's laurels, but can also be very expensive. Eventually, a return needs to be created on this investment via the valorization of the new and safeguarded IP.

Karl Marx (Figure 6.1) first introduced the term "valorization" in his work *Das Kapital*, which was published in 1867. The original word used was *Verwertung* or more specifically *Kapitalverwertung*. This term refers to the use or application of something so that it generates value. It is not that easily translated into other languages. The opposite term is *Entwertung*: the process where the capital value is decreased or the capital invested loses part or all of its value.

Figure 6.1 Karl Marx (1818–1883)

For valorization or *Verwertung*, it is important that a surplus value is created, i.e. an earning or a yield needs to be generated. Thus valorization of IP is creating a surplus value, an earning on that IP. The problem is how new IP can be used so that the capital value increases.

This can be done via different valorization routes/processes:

- a company or person can further develop the new IP into an article of commerce that can be sold
- a company or person can out-license the IP to another person or company that does the above
- a new company can be established that commercializes the new IP
- a company or person can refrain from turning the new IP into an article of commerce to maintain the value of an existing business.

The management of the valorization of new IP through these different routes is actually business development. Business development includes identifying and evaluating a possible business, and then realizing its full potential and full value.

Not all new IP can generate value, and a lot of new technologies and products fail in the market. It is important to assess thoroughly the value of newly created products, processes, services, and items subject to IP, even prior to protecting the possible new IP. Scientific curiosity will not always result in a commercially viable product. In addition, sufficient focus and effort need to be given to the valorization of new IP.

Baggott et al. (2008) reported that over a ten-year period (1991–2000) more than US$200 billion was invested in R&D at US-based universities, resulting in 1 million new disclosures, i.e. on average US$2 million per discovery. Approximately 50 percent were submitted for patent application, which yielded eventually 25,000 licenses. This resulted in the formation of 2,500 start-up companies, which often do not survive, and only 125 licenses that generate more than US$1 million per annum. Most of the licenses bring in just US$10,000 cumulatively. This is a rather sad return on investment and a significant waste of money (e.g. protecting the IP via a patent).

IP valuation

When in- or out-licensing a patent or commercializing it in general, it is important that the value of the patent is assessed. There are 20 main aspects to be considered.

1. Check whether the patent is in force.
2. Identify the context.
3. Gather information.
4. Assemble a valuation team.
5. Read the patent.
6. Investigate the patent's scope.
7. Talk with a patent attorney.
8. Inquire about the patent's validity.
9. Inquire into blocking patents.
10. Consider synergies among patents.
11. Investigate foreign patent protection.

12. Consider the remaining life of the patent.
13. Analyze any prior royalties paid for the patent.
14. Inquire into any actual or threatened litigation involving the patent.
15. Identify the next-best alternative technologies.
16. Estimate a demand curve for the patented item.
17. Determine the patented product's point of profit maximization.
18. Consider the applicability of traditional valuation approaches, e.g. net present value (NPV).
19. Do an income-approach valuation.
20. Write the patent valuation report.

How much is new IP worth? Is there a market for it? How much can we ask for the technology, product, or service? These questions need to be answered first, before you can start creating value on the new IP. The process of determining the value of an asset, IP, company, etc. is called valuation. There are many techniques for valuation, and it is often partially objective and partially subjective due to the estimations.

In this book, we mainly look at two different approaches:

- using industrial standards
- financial valuation via discounted cash flow (DCF) methods.

The methods and techniques presented are applicable for assessing the value of new IP within an existing company before initiating a project or when implementing project results. A company can also use these techniques to assess the value of IP when considering in-licensing, mergers, or acquisitions.

Industrial standards

Most likely, historical data exist on previous done deals in a specific industrial sector for a specific type of technology or product. These historical data can be found at different sources:

- established general terms and conditions for a specific industry
- surveys and business development literature

- licensing societies and business development communities
- journals and pay sites with databases
- consultants
- news and published agreements
- court cases.

Established industry norms

Using industry norms is a simple and easy approach requiring less effort compared to other approaches. The key is to find studies which are recent, since the established norms can evolve over time. There are different journals where information can be found, such as *Les Nouvelles*, *Licensing Economics Review*, *Journal of the Association of University Technology Managers*, *Review of Financial Economics*, and *International Review of Economics and Finance*.

Goldscheider et al. (2002) published a study on the royalty rates related to various industries for the period 1990–2000. As shown in Table 6.1, rates can vary significantly from industry to industry, but also within the same industry. The minimum and maximum can be wide apart. This is often due to the stage of development of the product or technology, the value of the technology, and of course the quality of the negotiators. Royalties are usually based on the generated net sales, although different possibilities exist – they can be included, for instance, in the transfer pricing if the licensor is producing the product for the licensee who sells it.

Table 6.1 Royalty rates for different industries, 2002

Industry	Av. oper. margin	*n* (no. of entries)	Min. royalty rate	Max. royalty rate	Median royalty rate
Automative	5.0%	35	1.0%	15.0%	4.0%
Chemicals	11.1%	72	0.5%	25.0%	3.6%
Computers	6.9%	68	0.2%	15.0%	4.0%
Food	7.3%	32	0.3%	7.0%	2.8%
Pharma & biotech	16.4%	328	0.1%	40.0%	5.1%
Software	18.8%	119	0.0%	70.0%	6.8%

Source: Goldscheider et al. (2002).

In a more recent study, Porter et al. (2008) reported royalty averages for the pharmaceutical, chemical, and medical device industries (Table 6.2).

Besides identifying the appropriate royalty rate, it is important to get a proper idea of what the different stage payments would be. Stage payments can include an upfront payment, i.e. after signing the agreement, or various payments when a critical milestone in product development or a certain target in sales has been reached. In most cases licensors (who sell the IP) prefer higher stage payments and lower royalties, whereas licensees (who buy the IP) prefer to agree on low stage payments and perhaps somewhat higher royalties. In general, the stage payments should be related to or cover the amount spent on development of the product or technology until the time it was licensed out.

More detailed information can be found by industrial sector. For instance, a vast amount of information can be found for the pharmaceutical industry. Table 6.3 gives an overview of the royalty rates and stage payments for products and technology at various stages of development.

Historical data on deals

More reliable detailed information for deal making can be obtained from available historical data on relevant deals that were closed in the past. The data studied need to be for a similar product or technology for a similar industrial sector.

Some of these data can be purchased from companies such as RoyaltyStat, Recap, Pharmadeals, Datamonitor, Life Science Analytics (www.medtrack.com), etc. This is often expensive, e.g. a subscription to RoyaltyStat costs US$4,500 per year with a maximum download of 100 deals per year.

Table 6.2 Royalty averages

Industry	Number of observations	Average royalty rate (%)	+/– (%)	Lower bound (%)	Upper bound (%)
Medical devices	77	4.35	0.64	3.71	5.00
Pharmaceutical	90	5.66	0.91	4.75	6.57
Chemical	21	3.70	0.88	2.82	4.57

Source: Porter et al. (2008).

Table 6.3 **Stage payments and royalties in the pharmaceutical industry**

Status	Type	Total stage payments (US$)	Royalty range (%ns)
Launched	Established	0	15–50
	New in area	0	10–30
Development	Discovery	1–20 million	2–8
	Preclinical	1–30 million	2–10
	Phase I or II	2–40 million	2–12
	Phase III	5–50 million	8–16
	Registration	20–60 million	8–20
Tech	Delivery system	1–15 million	1–10
	Platform	0.25–15 million	0.5–10
	Assays	25,000–100,000	none

Source: Scott (2005).

Let us look at an example of a pharmaceutical product for the treatment of respiratory tract infections in pre-clinical phase. The biotech company Advanced Life Sciences entered into an agreement with Abbott Laboratories on 1 December 2004 where Advanced Life Sciences acquired from Abbott a license to patents and proprietary technology related to the anti-infective ABT210. Details are presented in Table 6.4.

Table 6.4 **Deal terms regarding the anti-infective ABT210, 2004**

Stage	Pre-clinical phase
Licensor	Abbott Laboratories
Licensee	Advanced Life Sciences
Territory	Worldwide, excluding Japan
Deal type	Exclusive development license
Shares	282,763 shares go from licensee to licensor
Upfront payment	US$11 million
Stage payment	Yes, e.g. US$30 million upon US regulatory approval
Royalties	15% on net sales over US$200 million 16% on net sales over US$100 million 17% on net sales up to US$100 million

Source: Scott (2005).

Under the rules of the Securities and Exchange Commission (SEC) of the US government, public companies are required to disclose transactions that can have a significant effect on the value of the company, as a protection for shareholders. License agreements are often considered as having such a significant effect. There are SEC depositories where such agreements are filed and available to the public.

Besides information on license agreements, the SEC is also a great source to find more information on mergers and acquisitions, and on the value of goodwill. Goodwill is an intangible asset which provides a competitive advantage, such as a strong brand (trade names), company or product reputation, etc. Goodwill needs to be considered in the balance sheet by the acquirer besides the tangible assets. Let us illustrate this via an example of frozen pizzas. On 1 March 2010 the company Nestlé bought Kraft Foods' North American frozen pizza business for US$3.7 billion. The sale included the Di Giorno, Tombstone, and Jack's brands in the United States, the Delissio brand in Canada, and the California Pizza Kitchen trademark license. It also included two manufacturing sites and leases for pizza depots and delivery trucks. Kraft Foods (SIC code 2000: food and kindred products) reported in its Form-10-Q filing dated 6 August 2010 that net annual revenues for the frozen pizza business were approximately US$1.6 billion, resulting in annual earnings before income taxes of US$335 million. The US$3.7 billion sale price included tax expenses of US$1.2 billion and US$894 million in assets. Hence Nestlé paid approximately US$1.6 billion for the business itself, which equals five times the annual net earnings before taxes. How much was now actually paid for the goodwill, i.e. the brands/trademarks? This can be found in the details of the assets that were transferred: US$102 million for inventories, US$317 for property, plant, and equipment, and finally US$475 million for the goodwill. Thus it is worthwhile to protect trademarks and build strong brands.

Several publications provide details on closed deals, e.g. Porter et al. (2008) report on the clinical, pharmaceutical, and medical device industry. Companies that provide marketing studies also sell reports on licensing activities in a specific business. Global Business Insights released a study (Seget, 2006) on deal values in the pharmaceutical industry for various indicators (Figure 6.2).

The best deals were done in the area of oncology. As a comparison, the three best deals in oncology and the three best deals in the area of antivirals are presented in Table 6.5. These are numbers from more than ten years ago, which can be considered an eternity in business. Numbers can change very rapidly.

Figure 6.2 Average pharmaceutical deal values

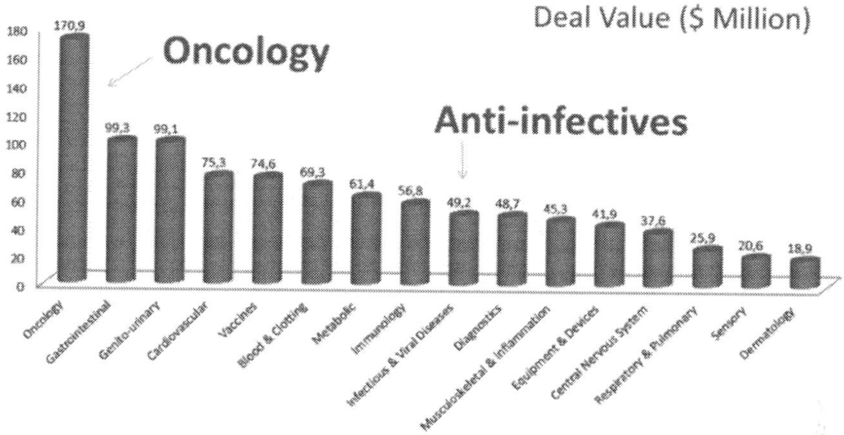

Source: Seget (2006).

Table 6.5 Top three deals on cancer and antivirus, 2002

Indication	Company 1	Company 2	Maximum deal value ($ million)
Cancer	Bristol-Myers Squibb	Imclone Systems	2,000.0
Cancer	Sanofi-Synthélabo	IDM	550.0
Cancer	Aventis	Genta	480.0
Antiviral	Roche	Stressgen	250.0
Antiviral	3M	Eli Lilly	100.0
Antibiotic	Hemispherx Biopharma	Laboratorios Del Dr. Esteve	98.0

Source: Global Business Insights (2002).

Court cases can also be an interesting source to estimate the value of technology. The company Innogenetics filed an application in 1993 on a hepatitis C genotyping and the patent was granted on 8 December 1998 (US 5846704). In September 2005 Innogenetics sued Abbott Laboratories, alleging that Abbott was infringing its patent.[1] On 1 September 2006 the court found that the patent was infringed as a matter of harm. This case is mentioned in several publications (e.g. FindLaw, undated), giving details of the US$7 million in damages Abbott had to pay Innogenetics:

- major diagnostic companies such as Roche, Bayer, and Third Wave Technologies had taken a license to this key patent
- the district court's damage award of US$7 million included a US$5.8 million market entry fee as well as an ongoing royalty of €5–10 per test.

This gives us an indication that for diagnostics in the field of hepatitis C, a non-exclusive license could include an upfront payment of US$5.8 million and ongoing royalties of €5–10 per test sold by the licensee.

Enhancing comparability

As mentioned, it is important to find industry norms or historical deal data related to your new IP in order to assess its value for e.g. licensing. Unfortunately, it is often difficult to find detailed information on deals which are very closely related to your IP. In addition, the market may have changed since the reference deal was closed, more competition could have entered the market, etc. The available information can be enhanced to match your specific case by means of a scoring system, a bit similar to scoring to evaluate a research project portfolio. The basis for this scoring is evaluating your IP on various pre-set criteria in relation to or comparison with the same criteria for products in historical related deals.

Criteria

First, the set of criteria must be determined. For licensing, most criteria relate to the IP position and strengths, deal type (e.g. exclusive versus non-exclusive), territory, patent remaining lifetime, advantages over old technology or products, number of competitors, sales and market potential, product costs, stage of development, and aspects of risk. A set of criteria often used in a legal context is the "15 Georgia Pacific factors".[2] Some sets of criteria can be very long and therefore rather impractical or cumbersome to use. An example is the 100-factor criteria list developed by Arnold and Headley (1987).

Scale

The next step is to choose a scale for the selected criteria, such as:

- a scale of 1–5, 1–7, or even 0–10, often referred to as a Likert scale
- a non-numerical scale such as "high, medium, low" or "–, =, +"
- other scales such as Crayola, where colors are used (white = neutral, green = better, blue = much better, orange = worse, and red = bad).

Weight

Not all criteria are equally important. Some could be more critical than others, and therefore a weight should be given to the criteria used. Sometimes a criterion can be so important that for instance a zero means that the overall score has to be zero, e.g. if a new pharmaceutical molecule cannot be patent protected, the actual value of the technology is nil since no company would invest large amounts of money to develop a medical product which can be copied later without a problem. This importance can be incorporated in the scoring by multiplying the individual weighted scores for each criterion, instead of adding them all up.

Scoring

Next the criteria, related scale, and weights are entered in a table or a graph and the new IP is scored for the perceived value of the criteria for the technology or product related to the reference deals or industry standards. This is best done by a team, to ensure that the average score is as objective as possible.

Adapting

After both the new IP and the technology/product have been scored, the numbers in the historical reference deals, or industrial standards, need to be adjusted based on the final overall score for the new IP versus the overall score for the technology or product related to the reference deal or industrial standard.

Let us illustrate this via an example. Previously (Table 6.4) we identified deal terms in 2004 on an anti-infective for the treatment of respiratory tract infections. Assuming we have a novel, patent-protected anti-infective in clinical phase 1 for the treatment of such infections, we want to assess a potential deal value for out-licensing. A possible scoring is presented in Table 6.6.

Table 6.6 An example of scoring to enhance comparability

Criteria	Scale					Weight	Score
Patent lifetime	1	2	3	**4**	5	2	8
Phase of development	1	2	3	4	**5**	2	10
Exclusivity	1	2	**3**	4	5	2	6
Competition	1	**2**	3	4	5	1	2
Advantage over others	1	2	**3**	4	5	1	3
Territory	1	2	3	**4**	5	1	4
Margins	1	2	3	**4**	5	1	4
Reference product = **3**						**Total**	**37**

The reference product as described in the deal would get a total score of 30. Our new product scored better in some areas, e.g. on stage of development and patent lifetime, resulting in a total score of 37.

We could define a correction factor as “the score for our product divided by the score of the reference product”. This correction factor can be used to determine estimated deal terms for our new proprietary anti-infective, as illustrated in Table 6.7.

These are of course estimates, and quite influenced by e.g. how a team perceives the value of its own new IP over competitor IP, often resulting in an overestimate. Additionally, if the new anti-infective in our example had scored the lowest for all criteria, giving the lowest overall score of 10, would the derived deal terms actually still be 33 percent (correction factor 10/30 = 0.33) worth of the deal terms of the reference product?

Table 6.7 An example of adapting historical deal terms (Table 6.4) to fit our new IP better

Term	Reference product	Correction factor	Our product
Upfront payment Stage payment	US$11 million US$30 million	$\frac{\text{score our product}}{\text{score ref. product}}$ = 37/30 = **1.23**	US$13.6 million US$37.0 million
Royalties			
Sales of US$200 million	15%		18.5%
Sales of US$100 million	16%	18.5%	19.7%
Sales <US$100 million	17%		21.0%

A somewhat more reliable estimate could be obtained if we are able to identify a very low-end deal and a very high-end deal for the related technology. In our example, if we have identified low- and high-end deals related to anti-infectives, our derived deal terms based on the scoring could look as shown in Table 6.8.

The term values for our anti-infective are determined by the formula:

our term value = *low-end term value* +
(high-end term value – *low-end term value)* ×
((our score – *minimum score)* /
(maximum score – *minimum score))*

If we are able to identify multiple related historical deals, we could work via another method to assess the possible value of our new IP: by clustering very closely related deals and ranking these clusters from low-end deals to the best possible deals. The deal characteristics (criteria) of each cluster can be studied and the new IP evaluated on each criterion/characteristic to see in which cluster it would fit best.

Let us continue with our previous example and imagine we are able to identify six related historical deals that we rank based on the royalty rate and stage payment. In a next step we study the deal terms in relation to a set of criteria to evaluate our new anti-infective on these criteria and see into which cluster it fits best (Table 6.9).

From the above we can conclude that for our new proprietary anti-infective we can expect between US$20 million and US$50 million in stage payments and 8–10 percent in royalties.

The "25 percent rule"

In the previous paragraphs we looked at established industrial standards/norms or historical related deals for estimating financial terms for the licensing out (or in) of new IP. What if no closely related standards or

Table 6.8 An example of enhancing comparability based on a deal window

Term	Low end (score 10)	High end (score 50)	Our technology
Upfront payment	US$5 million	US$20 million	US$15.13 million
Stage payment	US$20 million	US$80 million	US$60.5 million
Royalties	5%	20%	15.13%

Table 6.9 An example of clustering for obtaining deal terms

Deal	1	2	3	4	5	6
Stage payment (US$m)	5	15	20	50	60	80
Royalty (on net sales)	2–5%	5%	8%	10%	15%	20%
Patent lifetime		●	●	●		
Phase of development		●		●	●	
Exclusivity						
Competition	●	●				
Advantage over others			●	●		
Territory			●	●	●	●
Margins			●			

deals can be found? What could be an appropriate royalty for the new IP? A possible solution can be applying a general accepted rule of thumb, the "25 percent rule".

The rule, which is over 40 years old, is defined as "dividing the expected profits for the product or technology that incorporates the IP at issue in such a way that 25% is retained by the licensor (the seller) and that 75% goes to the licensee (the buyer)" (Goldscheider et al., 2002; Lu, 2011). The rule was initially used in valuing patents, but it can also be used in copyright, trademarks, trade secrets, and transfer of know-how.

New IP is assumed to be generating new sales in a specific business sector. After some research (e.g. internet, SEC, etc.) it is possible to identify relevant companies that are active in that sector, selling products or technology which are related to the new IP. If these related companies are public (in contrast to being private) it is quite easy to find details on their finances. Most public companies even publish their financial annual reports on their websites.

In these financial statements the turnover or revenue of the company is given and all related costs of doing business, such as:

- *COGS*: cost of goods sold, which is all directly related costs of producing the product, e.g. raw materials, direct related labor, depreciation of the experiment to make the product, etc.
- *sales and marketing*: expenses related to sales and/or marketing activities
- *R&D*: expenses for research and development
- *G&A*: general overheads and administration-related costs.

From these it is possible to calculate the company's earnings (Figure 6.3).

Another important factor is EBITDA, which is earnings or operational profit before interest, taxes, depreciation (of tangible fixed assets), and amortization (depreciation of non-tangible assets such as goodwill). Both depreciation and amortization are non-cash items. Hence EBITDA does not take into account the degree of contribution made by depreciation and amortization, and only focuses on the profitability of a company. It does not pay attention to the investment needed to obtain the profit. EBITDA is a good measure for analyzing businesses in the same industry where the capital-expenditure-to-revenue rates are often very similar.

For our 25 percent rule and estimating a royalty, we need the EBIT (earnings before interest and taxes) value. Why not the earnings after interest and taxes? This is quite obvious, since royalties paid by the licensee are a cost for the licensee and no taxes need to be paid, while royalties received by the licensor are considered income on which taxes need to be paid (except in certain countries, see below), and interest payments are not fixed annual reoccurring cash-out transactions.

EBIT can be expressed as a percentage of the original revenues. If we license out new IP that will result in sales of a new product in a specific business, it will result in revenues and, after all expenses, in EBIT. The 25 percent rule states that a licensor could ask for 25 percent of this EBIT.

Let us illustrate this via an example. It is quite difficult to find industrial norms or historical deal data on food- and agriculture-related *in vitro* diagnostics. Therefore, the 25 percent rule could help us estimate a good royalty rate for negotiations with possible licensees. After some inquiries and research, it is evident that Biomerieux is one of the important industrial players in this sector. Furthermore, Biomerieux

Figure 6.3 Calculating the earnings of a company

Turnover/sales/revenues – **COGS**
= gross margin – sales and marketing expenses – research and development – general overheads and administration – other expenses
= earnings/operational profit before interest and taxes (EBIT) – interest – taxes
= earnings/operational profit after interest and taxes

is a public company and on its website (www.biomerieux.com) a lot of financial data are available, including the annual report for 2009.

From this report we learn that net sales in 2009 reached €1,223.4 million, with 85 percent attributed to sales of clinical applications and 15 percent to sales of industrial applications, i.e. agri-food *in vitro* diagnostics. The industrial applications are currently growing at 9 percent per year. The figures are given in Table 6.10.

From the financials we learn that the EBIT (not including other operating income) in 2009 was €200.8 million, which is 16.4 percent of the net sales. If we apply the 25 percent rule, an appropriate royalty rate would be 25 percent of 16.4 percent = 4.10 percent on net sales related to new products based on the new IP. This is of course for all IP needed to get the products produced and sold. Indeed, if licenses to four different patents are actually needed and all the licensors apply the 25 percent rule, there will eventually be no earnings left for the licensee.

Studying the financials of companies active in the sector related to the area of a new innovation, product, or service can also help in determining the selling price of the new product. Determining the price is a very complicated and very important task. There are three main approaches: on a cost-plus base, based on prices of competitor products, or assessing the value of the product as perceived by the target customers. The last method is the most difficult and requires significant marketing and consumer research, but generally captures the best possible value. The

Table 6.10 Financial details of Biomerieux, 2009

Value		Percentage
Net sales	€1,223.4 million	100.0
Cost of goods (COGS)	– €563.8 million	– 46.0
Gross profit (gross margin)	**€659.6 million**	**54.0**
Other operating income	€12.5 million)	
Sales and marketing expenses	– €217.1 million	– 17.7
General and administration expenses	– €98.7 million	– 8.1
Research and development expenses	– €143.0 million	– 11.7
Total operating expenses	**– €458.8 million**	**– 37.5**
Operating income before non-recurring items (EBIT) minus other operating income	**– €200.8 million**	
Royalty on net sales **4.10%** ←	25 percent rule ←	**16.4**

first two are easier and often used for me-too or commodity products. For a new product you can calculate and determine the full burdened cost (COGS) for production, and a possible selling price can then be defined by dividing the calculated cost by the COGS percentage from a company active in the sector.

In addition, licensees can argue that licensors should retain less than 25 percent because:

- the product is in an early stage of development
- very large investments are required in order to manufacture the product
- the business operates with small margins in a very competitive environment
- the technological and economic risks are very high.

On the other hand, licensors can argue that the licensee should get less than 75 percent because:

- the product or technology is at the end of development, ready to be produced
- the majority of the technological and economic risk has been taken away
- the product is superior compared to others, and it is a strong-growing market
- the COGS is very low and the selling price high, resulting in excellent margins
- the licensee's competitor is offering better terms.

It is important to compare the EBIT numbers from several players in the sector, since these can differ significantly. This means that a more reliable royalty estimate can be obtained by averaging the EBIT values and applying the 25 percent rule to this average. Even in a traditional sector such as the food industry, EBIT can vary widely. An overview of some major food enterprises for the year 2009 is given in Table 6.11.

There is quite a difference between the lowest calculated royalty rate, 2.59 percent for Grupo Bimbo, and the highest calculated royalty rate of 4.49 percent for General Mills. This indicates that licensing negotiations with Grupo Bimbo could be "very different" to licensing negotiations with General Mills. As with industrial norms and historical deal data,

Table 6.11 **Food companies' EBIT numbers, 2009**

Company	Revenue* (€ million)	EBIT* (€ million)	As % of revenue	% royalty on net sales**
Nestlé	71,270	10,397	14.6	3.65
Unilever	39,823	5,020	16.6	3.15
Kraft	28,971	3,963	13.7	3.42
General Mills	10,539	1,894	18.0	4.49
Grupo Bimbo	6,233	646	10.4	2.59
Heinz	7,182	1,078	15.0	3.70
Campbell's	5,442	850	15.6	3.90
			Av. 14.84	3.56

*Conversions are based on weighted average annual rates.

**Calculated as 25 percent of the EBIT.

the scoring approach described earlier in this chapter can help to enhance the calculated value for your specific new IP.

We have described the use of the 25 percent rule for revenues generated on new proprietary products. What about new IP on processes that allow the production of known products, but at a significantly lower price (COGS) compared to known production processes? The 25 percent rule will not be applied to the revenues generated by the already commercialized product, but on the gain resulting from the proprietary improved production process over the old process.

For instance, a diagnostic kit is sold for €100 and the production cost (COGS) using the known process is €40, giving a gross margin of €60. If we have a new proprietary process that allows us to produce the same kit for only €25, the gross margin increases to €75, a difference of €15. On this difference we can apply the 25 percent rule. Thus a licensor owning a process-based IP could propose to the licensee who currently sells the diagnostic kits a royalty of 0.25 x €15 = €3.75 per kit sold, or calculated as a proportion of the selling price of the kit €3.75 / €100 = 3.75 percent royalty on the sale price.

Besides the 25 percent rule, some other helpful rules of thumb exist.

- Deal term values for non-exclusive licenses are half or less compared to deal terms for exclusive licenses.
- For upfront/stage payments, 5–10 percent of the total retained intrinsic value is an appropriate number, just as one would pay 5–10 percent in advance when buying a car, furniture, etc.

- For fully developed or already commercialized products, split profit is very appropriate.
- Upfront payment should at a minimum cover all IP-related costs.

In the last couple of years a lot of debate and controversy has arisen around the 25 percent rule, after the *Uniloc* case in which the use of the rule was barred.[3] Kidder and O'Brien (2011) are quite bold in stating that the rule is simply wrong, and provide arguments for that. Jarczyk (2011) commented after the *Uniloc* ruling that a more defensible approach for determining royalty rates may involve the examination of third-party license agreements that are sufficiently similar to the subject.

Alternatives to the 25 percent rule are being developed and proposed, such as an investment-based method for determining fair, reasonable, and non-discriminatory (FRAND) licensing royalties.

FRAND licensing royalties

This method is based on the accounting principle of return on investment (ROI). This is defined as follows:

$$\begin{aligned} \text{ROI} &= C_{\text{return}} / I_{\text{investment}} \\ &= (\text{gain of investment} - \text{cost of investment}) / \text{cost of investment} \end{aligned}$$

Granstrand and Holgersson (2012) argue that fair, reasonable, and non-discriminatory licensing terms to potential licensees should be based on equalizing the rates of ROI for the parties involved. In principle the returns from a licensing deal should be shared among the involved actors in proportion to their respective investments. FRAND can be applied to situations where a single licensor and a single licensee need to be considered, but also in cases with multiple licensors and licensees. For a bilateral agreement the following formula can be applied:

$$L = \frac{Is}{Ib + Is} \pi OPh$$

where:
L = royalties paid by licensee
Is = investment by the licensor (seller)
Ib = investment by the licensee (buyer)
πOPh = operating profit of the licensee.

For multiple parties a more complex formula can be used:

$$\mathrm{Lik} = \mathrm{Li}\ \frac{\mathrm{Isk}}{\mathrm{Is}} = \pi\mathrm{OPhi} - \frac{\mathrm{Ibi}}{\mathrm{Ib} + \mathrm{Is}} \pi\mathrm{OPh}\ \frac{\mathrm{Isk}}{\mathrm{Is}}$$

where:
Lik = royalty from licensee I to licensor k
Li = license royalty payments
πOPhi = operating profit from licensee i
Isk = investments by licensor k
Is = total licensors' investments
Ib = total licensees' investments
Ibi = investment by licensee i
πOPh = total operating profit from licensees.

Let us look at an example where a food-related new product is developed. Assume the licensor took the initiative to start a project, established a proof of concept, and contacted a major food producer such as Unilever. The licensor invested €2.5 million on basic research, while the licensee (Unilever) continued with the development and invested €5 million. The operating profit for Unilever is 16.6 percent. The royalty according to FRAND should be:

$$\mathrm{L} = \frac{2.5\,\mathrm{million}}{5\,\mathrm{million} + 2.5\,\mathrm{million}} 16.6\% = 5.53\%\ \text{on net sales}$$

Using the 25 percent rule, we would propose 3.56 percent. The FRAND rule is at its core more interesting for the licensor, but there are some problems or concerns. At the start of a project, the risk is much higher than when progress has been made and the project is moving towards commercialization. Investments made at an early stage with a higher risk should be rewarded more than investments made in a later stage where the risk is much less. Also, if a licensor invested everything and can offer a ready-to-sell product to a licensee, using the FRAND rule all of the operating profit should go to the licensor. The licensee will definitely not be happy with such an agreement. In practice, in this case often a split-profit agreement is put in place.

Discounted cash flow methods

The previous methods are more general and somewhat empirical; the DCF method is much more mathematical. The DCF method and related elaborated systems such as Monte Carlo simulations or real options are the commonest approaches in industry, used by business developers to assess the value of IP and related transactions.

The basic concept is quite simple: suppose you have a monthly net salary of €2,500 which you can use to buy food, drinks, clothing, etc. If you have the same salary ten years from now, you would notice that you could buy much less compared to today. Everything would have become more expensive, and your amount of money is actually worth less due to inflation.

The DCF method calculates via discounting what the actual value would be today, i.e. the present-time value, of the €2,500 you would have ten years from now. This method gives you the net present value.

The DCF equation

To calculate NPV values, three important inputs are required:

- a value, cash (c)
- a period of time (t)
- the rate at which a value is decreasing in time related to inflation, risk, etc. – this is called the discount rate (d).

For this calculation we need an equation for converting future cash payments into their present equivalent, taking into account the time when these payments are made and the risk, inflation, etc. associated with them.

If we put our €2,500 (m) into a savings account with an interest rate (i) of 2.70 percent (e.g. Deutsche Bank in January 2011), after one year our investment would be worth (v).

$$v = m + (i \times m)$$

Value one year from now

$= €2,500 + (0.027 \times €2,500) = €2,500 + €67.5 = €2,567.5$

Value two years from now

$= €2,567.5 + (0.027 \times €2,567.5) = €2,636.8$

Or

$$\begin{aligned} v &= (m + (i \times m)) + (m + (i \times m)) \times i \\ &= m \times (1 + i) + m \times (1 + i) \times i \\ &= m \times (1 + i) \times (1 + i) \\ &= m \times (1 + i)^2 \end{aligned}$$

Continuing for three years, an additional factor of (1 + i) needs to be added, for four years, two more factors, etc. The generalized formula can be derived as:

$$v_n = m \times (1+i)^n$$

This is the value n years from now, with (vn) the total value at year n after an initial amount of money (m) invested at an interest rate of (i).

For instance, our €2,500 invested now would be worth €3,263.2 in ten years from now. However, with the DCF method we want to do the reverse, i.e. calculating the present value (m) of a known future amount (vn). We can transform the above equation to:

$$m = \frac{v_n}{(1+i)^n}$$

In this case our interest rate actually needs to be the discount rate (d). In the financing community worldwide, the generally accepted term for "m" is present value (PV) and for "vn" is cash at year n (Cn). This gives the generally recognized function:

$$PV = \frac{c_n}{(1+d)^n}$$

Referring to our example of a monthly net salary of €2,500 in ten years from now, we can use this equation to calculate what this €2,500 would be worth. If we set d at 2.5 percent, being the average inflation rate in the European Union for 2010 (Trading Economics, 2010), the PV of €2,500 received ten years from now is:

$$PV = \frac{€2{,}500}{(1+0.025)^{10}}$$

$$PV = €1{,}953$$

This equation determines the PV of a single amount of cash received n years from now. When we want to commercialize new IP, we expect not just one amount of cash in one given year, but several amounts of cash (in or out) for multiple years. During the first years we can face significant investments for development, and after commercialization hopefully several years of sales, resulting in some earnings (cash in) after covering all expenses. The sum of these net amounts of cash in a given year *n*, discounted over a period of n years, gives us the NPV of the commercialized new IP. This gives us the final equation:

$$NPV = \sum_{t=0}^{n} \frac{Cn}{(1+d)^{n}}$$

Depending on the series of cash flows, the discount rate, and the period of time, the NPV value can be:

- positive, meaning that one could get earnings from the investment
- zero, meaning that all earnings will cover all investments, giving you a net of zero
- negative – you will invest more money than you earn, resulting in an overall loss.

If we have a positive NPV, we can determine what discount rate would render the initial NPV to zero. This value for "d" is defined as the internal rate of return (IRR):

$$\sum_{t=0}^{n} \frac{Ct}{(1+d)^{t}} = 0$$

The IRR value can be compared to a pre-set minimum, i.e. the rate of a minimum return/yield:

- if the IRR is higher, the product or technology gives a better return than expected
- if the IRR is lower, the product or technology gives a lower return than expected and could be abandoned.

The cash flow projections

Determining the NPV requires determining the cash flows for the different years that are part of the NPV calculation. Generally the period considered is the remaining lifespan of the product or technology, or in most cases of the patent (20 years). It is of course impossible to look into the future, so all numbers are estimations and the cash flows are *pro forma* (Figure 6.4). Nevertheless, it is important to use solid data and make the estimations as reliable as possible. One must be able to defend and explain the values used.

To obtain a net cash flow for a specific year, one needs to estimate the revenue and all related costs for that year. There are two main approaches.

- *Bottom up:* you analyze the total market, market growth, competitors, targeted group of customers, market share, and price setting, based on which you determine/estimate the revenue for a specific year. In addition, you calculate all expected related costs for the required activities (research and development, sales and marketing, capital expenditure/depreciation, production, etc.) for a year (often referred to as activity-based costing), and the total is then subtracted from the revenue to give the net cash for that year.
- *Top down:* you use the current overall market for the product, growth expectations, and annual sales of related existing products to estimate annual revenues. For costs and expenses you can use industry averages for the different categories, expressed as a percentage of the annual revenues, which are subtracted from the estimated revenues to give the net cash flow for a specific year.

Figure 6.5 gives an example of revenue income from a top-down perspective and a bottom-up approach.

It is also possible to combine items from both main approaches to derive your *pro forma* cash flow for calculating the NPV. The bottom-

Figure 6.4 Cash flow projection to calculate the NPV

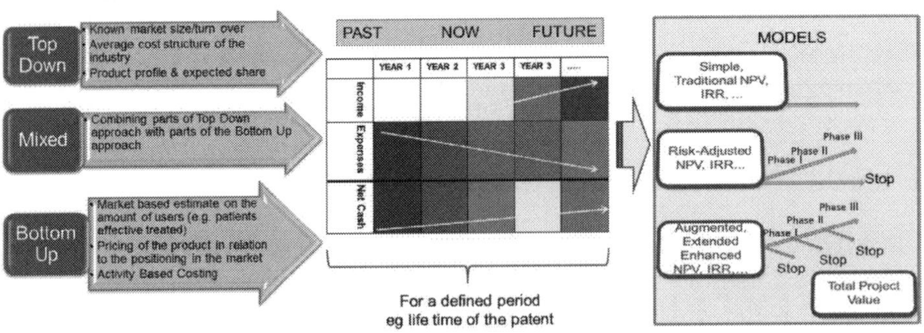

Figure 6.5 An example of an income/revenue *pro forma*

TOP DOWN

(€ million)	Year 1	Year 2	Year 3	Year ...	Year ...
Total Market	100	104	110	116	123
Market share*	0,5%	1%	2%	3%	4%
Sales*	0,5	1,04	2,20	3,48	4,92

BOTTOM UP

(€ million)	Year 1	Year 2	Year 3	Year ...	Year ...
# of customers*	20000	30000	50000	80000	110000
# purchases /customers*	1	1	2	2	3
Volume*	20000	30000	100000	160000	330000
Price/unit	€ 5	€ 5,25	€ 5,60	€ 6,00	€ 6,50
Sales*	€ 100000	€ 157500	€ 560000	€ 960000	€ 2145000

*expected

up approach can be very cumbersome, requiring a lot of effort and time. For our valorization efforts the top-down approach is very appropriate, although including some elements of the bottom-up method can result in more reliable projections.

Where can we find numbers on revenues, annual sales of related products, market trends/growth, and market share of relevant players?

- The internet.
- Annual reports of related businesses (their websites).
- Yahoo Finance.
- www.google.com/finance.
- Form-10 submissions of business-related companies (www.SEC.gov).
- Eurostat (EU), NASS or USDA (US), NBSC (China), MOSPI (India), BGE (Brazil), etc.
- Websites of the Food and Agriculture Organization, World Health Organization, OECD, Centers for Disease Control, etc.
- Business databases such as MedTrack, IMS, Datamonitor, Recap, Reuters, Global Business Insights, etc. (mostly on a fee basis).
- Marketing reports that can be purchased from Frost and Sullivan, Euromonitor, Global Business Insights, Datamonitor, Reportlinker, MarketResearch, etc.
- Business newspapers and trade magazines.

The compound annual growth rate (CAGR) can be estimated/based on the increase in revenues in the current year over previous years. More reliable CAGRs can be obtained via marketing studies.

As discussed earlier, costs or expenses as a percentage of revenues/turnover are shown in the financials of business-related companies. These financial reports are readily available for public companies and can be found easily:

- annual reports on the company's website
- www.SEC.gov (Form-10K)
- www.google.com/finance
- marketing studies from various providers.

Google Finance is quite interesting, since it allows you to find competitors and compare various financial parameters easily. It is important of course to ensure that the data are relevant and correct. Procter & Gamble is active in various businesses (consumer products, personal care, pharmaceuticals, etc.), thus you cannot use cost estimates based on the consolidated financials of P&G for e.g. a pharmaceutical-related product. The data used need to be as closely related as possible to your new IP and business sector. Therefore it is often necessary to average values from competitor companies or build in cross-checks in deriving your profit and loss statement estimations. Care must be taken when using financials of small and/or start-up companies, since the first years of business require much investment, so the initial EBIT values can be negative. It is better to use data of related companies that have been somewhat longer in business and are well established.

The differences between expenses (costs) and capital expenditures/investments can be confusing, and some clarification may be helpful. The first type of cost concerns actual, full expenses related to producing the product (COGS), selling it, etc. The second type of cost is related to large investments that need to be made in e.g. buildings, equipment (tangible assets), or goodwill (intangible assets). Such capitalized expenses for long-lined assets are "written down" via rules of depreciation (for tangible assets) over a period of time allowed by governing tax law, e.g. 20 years for buildings, seven years for equipment, and two years for computer/ICT hardware. Hence in the income statement for a specific year only a part of the total capital expenditure is taken up, i.e. the depreciation and/or amortization. The big lines are presented in Table 6.12.

Table 6.12 The big lines of a profit and loss statement

Total annual sales (also called revenues, turnover) – Cost of goods sold (COGS)
= **Gross margin** – Sales and marketing costs/expenses – Research and development costs/expenses – General overhead and administration expenses = **Earnings before interest, taxes, depreciation, and amortization (EBITDA)** – Depreciation (tangible assets) – Amortization (intangible assets)
= **Earnings before interest and taxes (EBIT)** (also called operational profit before interest and taxes) – Interest – Provision for taxes
= **Earnings after taxes** (also called operational profit after taxes)

Our *pro forma* with cash projections can be divided into two sub-periods: before product launch and after product launch. Sales can only be expected after product launch; before this we are mainly facing costs.

Post-launch we can assume that revenues gradually increase to a maximum of the estimated total sales potential in any one year, thus reaching the maximum annual sales. The total sales potential for a specific year can increase further in following years, based on the CAGR, or decrease if more competitive products enter the market and the product is getting old. A possible gradual increase of revenues after launch can be:

- one year after launch – 5 percent of estimated total annual sales potential
- two years after launch – 20 percent of estimated total annual sales potential
- three years after launch – 40 percent of estimated total annual sales potential
- four years after launch – 70 percent of estimated total annual sales potential
- five years after launch – 100 percent of estimated total annual sales potential.

Sales of new products follow a typical S-curve (if they do not fail). Growth of sales has been studied very intensively and some researchers have derived mathematical functions, e.g. the Gompertz curve and the Fisher-Pry model.

As mentioned, for NPV calculation a time period is used that covers the product/technology lifespan and the patent lifetime (20 years). In most cases the sales at the end of this period do not stop abruptly (e.g. the product is taken out of the market), but continue for some time. It is also not practical to forecast cash flows for an infinite number of future years. Therefore a terminal value (TV) is added after the final year, which is a rough estimate of all cash flows thereafter. An estimate is fine, since cash flows that are very far off in the future are less important, less significant. Several mathematical equations exist for TV, but the most commonly used is:

$$TV = \frac{Ctv}{d(1+d)^t}$$

If constant cash flows continue after the period considered, the constant TV (CTV) is identical to the cash flow of the last year of that period, but often it can be a reduced number as sales decline. For instance, in the pharmaceutical industry, after a patent expires, generic products are allowed on the market, reducing the market share and sales of the previously patent-protected product to approximately 20 percent or less

Figure 6.6 Decreased sales after patent expiry

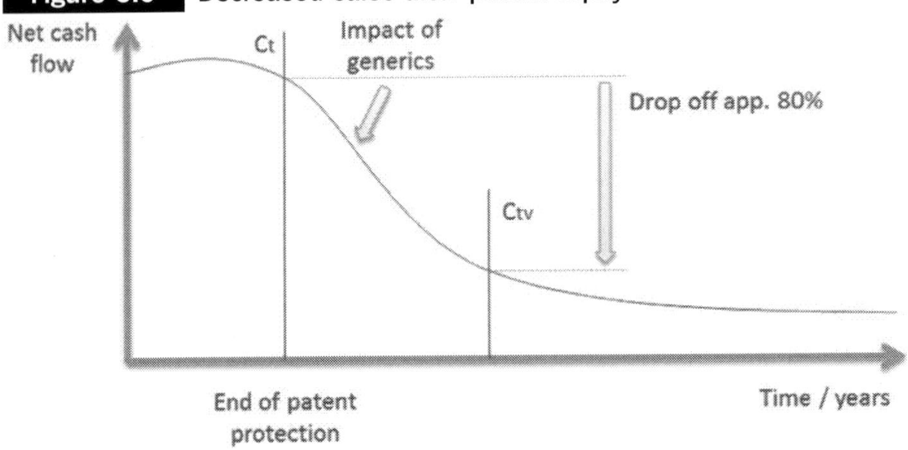

of what they used to be (Figure 6.6). Hence in this case the value of CTV is set at 20 percent of the cash flow of the last year.

From a cost perspective, we can use the ratios as derived previously. We still include the general depreciation and amortization, maintaining a total constant asset value. Moreover, investments need to continue to keep buildings, equipment, etc. in state-of-the-art conditions.

Before launching the product or technology, investments are needed to produce the product (in existing buildings with free space or new buildings; using existing equipment with free machine time or new equipment), plus additional investments to complete R&D, develop sales channels, spend on advertising and marketing, etc. By analyzing multiple business sectors and related companies over multiple time periods, it is possible to make reasonable approximations of such costs. Here, experience and expertise are truly important. Besides internal expertise, you can look for outside expertise and experience via consultants or even the licensee. For some business sectors in-depth studies are available, e.g. costings and required time to complete different phases of product development in the pharmaceutical industry. Parexel International publishes such data on a regular basis, and also scientific/business literature can be a source of information (DiMasi et al., 2003; Grabowski et al., 2002).

During the decade leading up to 2000 it was shown that clinical development costs increased at a rate of 11.8 percent per annum in constant 2000 dollar values. It is clear that clinical trials became larger over that decade, and this increase in costs seems broadly reasonable. Over the same ten-year period, average peak drug sales increased at a rate of 2.9 percent per annum. The smaller rise in sales compared to drug development costs is understandable given the continued rise of healthcare cost-containment measures across major markets and the impact of aggressive generic competition on prices. According to a study in Global Business Insights (Segret, 2006), to calculate cost and revenue levels, a general inflation rate must be included alongside the price increases in constant dollar amount, estimated to be a further 3 percent per annum. For example, the 2010 cost of a phase I trial expressed in 2010 dollars involves calculating ten years of price increases as a result of increased trial costs (11.8 percent) as well as accounting for the change in dollar value from 2000 to 2010 dollars (3 percent per annum – Table 6.13). The resulting sum is as follows:

2000 phase I trial cost (2000 dollars) × (1 + 11.8% + 3%) ^ 2010
= 2010 phase I trial cost (2010 dollars)

Table 6.13 **Several pharmaceutical-related input parameters for DCF models**

	Cost US$, 2000	Cost US$, 2010	Duration (months)	Probability of success	Probability to launch
Discovery	Not available	Not available	Not available	0.01%	0.01%
Pre-clinical	5.2 million	20.7 million	12.0	33%	1%
Phase I	15.2 million	46.4 million	12.3	81%	10% (phases I+II)
Phase II	23.5 million	71.7 million	26.0	58%	10% (phases I+II)
Phase III	86.3 million	263.3 million	33.8	57%	80%
Registration	2.0 million	6.1 million	18.2	92%	100%
Phase IV	140.0 million	472.1 million	36.0	100%	100%

Once the 2010 levels for all key costs and revenues have been established, the real increase in these values over time must be added to the model. Costs and revenues remain in 2010 dollar values, but the real increases in costs and revenues (11.8 percent and 2.9 percent per annum respectively) must also be extrapolated. Obviously, for the years after 2010 similar cost increases need to be considered. Via marketing studies, one can obtain a better view of the actual growth rate (CAGR) for a specific product class until a specific determined point in time.

In this way, all costs and revenues are expressed in a common, constant value measure and reflect the real levels of increase in costs and values that will occur over time. Hence all figures can be added together to represent a more reliable true total value. It is important to point out that the base case model must involve cost and revenue projections that account for real increases over time and are expressed in a common value measure (e.g. 2010 dollars) to allow a real valuation aggregation.

More detailed information can be gathered via inquiring (asking for quotations) with suppliers of equipment, contractors, toll manufacturers, contract research organizations, advertising companies, contracted sales organizations, etc.

As a simplistic approach, some rules of thumb can again be used (Razgaitis, 2009).

- Total cost prior to launch can be assumed to be similar to 50 percent or 100 percent of the first year of maximum annual sales, depending on the relevant industrial sector.

- For capital expenditure an assumption can be made based on (up to) 50 percent of the total cost prior to launch, which is depreciated over a period of ten years and the related depreciations are taken up in the *pro forma* until launch (remember that post-launch we included depreciations and amortizations in our earlier derived ratios).

Let us clarify all the above with two examples. A biotech company has done some basic research and developed a new drug candidate for the treatment of ocular allergy, OCAL-1. What would a *pro forma* profit and loss or income statement look like? What would be the intrinsic value of this new IP?

A quick search on the internet gives us Alcon as one of the important companies active in the area of ophthalmics. Continuing the search (e.g. Google Finance) will bring you some competitors – Novartis, Bauch & Lomer, Allergan, etc. The financials of Allergan for 2008, found in its annual report (www.allergan.com) and its SEC filings (www.SEC.gov), state that the total worldwide ophthalmic market was estimated to be US$12.5 billion and growing at an average of 9 percent per year. The income statement for Alcon in 2008 is given in Table 6.14.

From Alcon's annual report for 2009 we learn that its sales that year were US$6.5 billion, which is 6.3 percent more compared to US$6.29 billion in 2008. Approximately 18 percent of Alcon's sales come from products to treat ocular allergy. The sales increase for this category was 5.5 percent over 2008. Alcon's product Pataday® is the most prescribed drug worldwide for the treatment of ocular allergy, and in 2009 it generated US$355 million in sales.

Not all products for ocular allergy generate sales like Pataday. Acular® from Allergan only did US$86 million in 2009. If we compare product

Table 6.14 Profit and loss for Alcon, 2008

	Million US$	As % of sales
Sales	**6,294**	**100.0**
COGS	1,472	23.4
Gross profit	**4,822**	**76.6**
Sales, general overheads, and administration	1,961	31.2
R&D	619	9.8
Amortization	29	0.4
Operating income	**2,213**	**35.2**

characteristics (e.g. safety profile, ease of use, efficacy), we estimate that our new proprietary product OCAL-1 is more related to Pataday than to Acular. Hence we will use the sales of Pataday in 2009 as assumed top worldwide annual sales for OCAL-1. Once again we could use the scoring system to estimate where OCAL-1 might be positioned in sales compared to Pataday or Acular.

Let us assume that the patent on OCAL-1 was filed in 2009, hence we will develop a *pro forma* for the period 2009–2028. From Parexel's handbook on R&D statistics (Mathieu, 2008), we learn that for this type of pharmaceuticals it takes approximately six years to finish clinical development and an additional year for registration, i.e. seven years before we can commercialize the product. Hence we can launch OCAL-1 at the end of 2016 or the beginning of 2017. We assume that after launch sales will increase gradually until they reach the assumed top annual sales of US$355 million.

As a CAGR thereafter, we estimate 5.5 percent, similar to the growth rate for Pataday in 2009. As pre launch costing for investments in equipment, machines, and infrastructure we use the rule of thumb and take 50 percent of the maximum annual sales, spread over a period of ten years (depreciation). This value will be used for operational/production costs until launch. In this case we actually calculated the pre-launch costing (bottom-up approach), which was quite low because existing equipment and infrastructure could be used. Afterwards, depreciations are incorporated in the calculated ratios for expenses, as shown in Table 6.14.

We assume that all discovery work on OCAL-1 has finished, and cost US$5 million. Basic pre-clinical work started in 2010 and will continue in 2011. Assume that we are now in the year 2011 and will need to start discounting in 2012. It is easy to make a financial model in Excel, and an overview of the NPV calculation is given in Figure 6.7.

As you can see, the resulting NPV of US$500 million is very high and the related IRR is 13 percent. These kinds of numbers are quite common in the pharmacy industry. Keep in mind that this is a *pro forma* and we estimated (or owners of IP often hope) that the new product will do as well as the top-selling product with the highest market share, in a growing market. What would the numbers look like if our new IP did not do as well as Pataday, but much less, e.g. similar to the Allergan product Acular, with sales in 2009 of US$86 million? Recalculating the whole model based on this value gives us a negative NPV of –US$280 million! The whole project would not be worth doing.

Figure 6.7 An NPV calculation for OCAL-1

OCAL-1 for Ocular Allergy

Costs (US$)	Probability of success*	2009	2010	2011	2012	2013	2014	2015	2016
Discovery	100.00%	5.000.000							
Preclinical	33%		10.336.946	11.868.813					
Phase I	81%			25.922.294	28.981.125				
Phase II	58%				44.806.344	50.093.493			
Phase III	57%					122.640.239	137.111.787	137.111.787	
Registration	92%								11.915.132
Total		5.000.000	10.336.946	37.789.107	73.787.469	172.733.731	137.111.787	137.111.787	11.915.132
Marketing/Sales								5.000.000	15.000.000
from 2017 as % revenu (SG&A)***	31%								
R&D as a % of revenue***	10%								
COGS (investments building & equipment)								5.000.000	5.000.000
from 2017 as a % of revenu***	23%								

* Parexel's statistics 2006/2007

** Pharmaceutical Licensing Strategies, GlobalBusinessInsights, 2006.

US$ Equiv.**	2009	2010	2011	2012	2013	2014	2015	2016	2017	2018
Preclinical	5.200.000	20.873.891	23.733.827	27.248.204	31.278.642	35.967.881	41.222.247	47.323.140	54.328.965	62.367.353
Phase I	15.200.000	46.372.619	51.844.588	57.962.249	64.801.795	72.448.407	80.997.318	90.555.002	101.240.492	113.186.870
Phase II	23.500.000	71.694.509	80.154.462	89.612.668	100.186.985	112.009.060	125.226.117	140.002.799	156.523.130	174.992.859
Phase III	86.300.000	263.286.645	294.354.470	329.088.297	367.920.716	411.335.361	459.872.933	514.137.939	574.806.216	642.633.350
Registration	2.000.000	6.101.660	6.821.668	7.626.612	8.526.552	9.532.686	10.657.542	11.915.132	13.321.117	14.893.009

Sales		
Top sales in US$ (2009 numbers)***	based on Pataday (US$)	355.000.000
Sales Annual Growth Rate***	5,50%	
Top sales continue for 5 years		
Afterwards yearly decrease of	5%	
Penetration until maximum share	5% in 2017	
	10% in 2018	
	25% in 2019	
	50% in 2020	
	75% in 2021	
	100% in 2022	
Terminal value as a % of the Discounted Net Cash last year		20%

***Annual Report Alcon 2010

** Pharmaceutical Licensing Strategies, GlobalBusinessInsights, 2006.

Discount rate	8%
Patent filed	2009
Product launch	2017

Project Year	2009	2010	2011	2012	2013	2014	2015	2016	2017	2018
Sales Potential (prescription)	355.000.000	374.525.000	395.123.875	416.855.688	439.782.751	463.970.802	489.489.196	516.411.102	544.813.713	574.778.467
Sales	0	0	0	0	0	0	0	0	27.240.686	57.477.847
COGS	0	0	0	0	0	0	5.000.000	5.000.000	6.374.320	13.449.816
SG&A	0	0	0	0	0	0	5.000.000	15.000.000	8.499.094	17.933.088
R&D	5.000.000	10.336.946	37.789.107	73.787.469	172.733.731	137.111.787	137.111.787	11.915.132	2.669.587	5.632.829
Net cash	-5.000.000	-10.336.946	-37.789.107	-73.787.469	-172.733.731	-137.111.787	-147.111.787	-31.915.132	9.697.684	20.462.113
Discounted cash	-5.000.000	-10.336.946	-37.789.107	-68.321.730	-148.091.333	-108.843.757	-108.131.555	-21.720.902	6.111.186	11.939.447
Accumulated discounted net cash	-5.000.000	-15.336.946	-53.126.053	-121.447.783	-269.539.117	-378.382.874	-486.514.429	-508.235.331	-502.124.145	-490.184.699

Project Year	2019	2020	2021	2022	2023	2024	2025	2026	2027	2028	TV
Sales Potential (prescription)	606.391.283	639.742.803	674.928.657	712.049.734	751.212.469	792.529.155	836.118.258	882.104.762	930.620.524	981.804.653	
Sales	151.597.821	319.871.402	506.196.493	712.049.734	751.212.469	792.529.155	836.118.258	882.104.762	930.620.524	932.714.421	
COGS	35.473.890	74.849.908	118.449.979	166.619.638	175.783.718	185.451.822	195.651.672	206.412.514	217.765.203	218.255.174	
SG&A	47.288.520	99.799.877	157.933.306	222.159.517	234.378.290	247.269.096	260.868.897	275.216.686	290.353.604	291.006.899	
R&D	14.856.686	31.347.397	49.607.256	69.780.874	73.618.822	77.667.957	81.939.589	86.446.267	91.200.811	91.406.013	
Net cash	53.988.824	113.874.219	180.205.952	253.489.705	267.431.639	282.140.379	297.658.100	314.029.295	331.300.907	332.046.334	630.115.834
Discounted cash	29.157.675	56.965.460	83.470.223	108.717.390	106.200.783	103.742.432	101.840.987	98.995.131	96.703.577	89.741.814	207.735.682
Accumulated discounted net cash	-461.027.022	-404.061.562	-320.591.338	-211.873.949	-105.673.166	-1.930.734	99.410.253	198.405.383	295.108.960	384.850.774	592.586.456

NPV	592.586.456
IRR	13%

Another important fact to consider is that in our example the proprietary product OCAL-1 is in an early phase of clinical development and the chances of eventually launching the product are extremely low. If we risk adjust the NPV value, it would be much lower. We can use the discount rate to take into account the overall risk of the project. The NPV in our previous example can vary significantly depending on the discount rate "d" used, as shown in Figure 6.8.

The business risk associated with realizing the stream of expected cash flow may be captured through the use of appropriate discount rates, which are industry-specific and/or linked to the development stage of a novel technology. This is explained in the next section. The major drawback is the chance of error due to subjective estimation. The DCF approach also does not account for the different risks and uncertainties associated with multistage cash flow and variable discount rates over the lifetime of a patent, hence the valuation of the patent has to be split into several distinct phases. Therefore, several risk-adjusted DCF methods have been developed: two very basic examples are the risk-adjusted discount rate (RADR) NPV and the certainty equivalent (CE) method (Hillier et al., 2010; Baker and English, 2011).

Figure 6.8 NPV values for the OCAL-1 example, depending on discount rate used

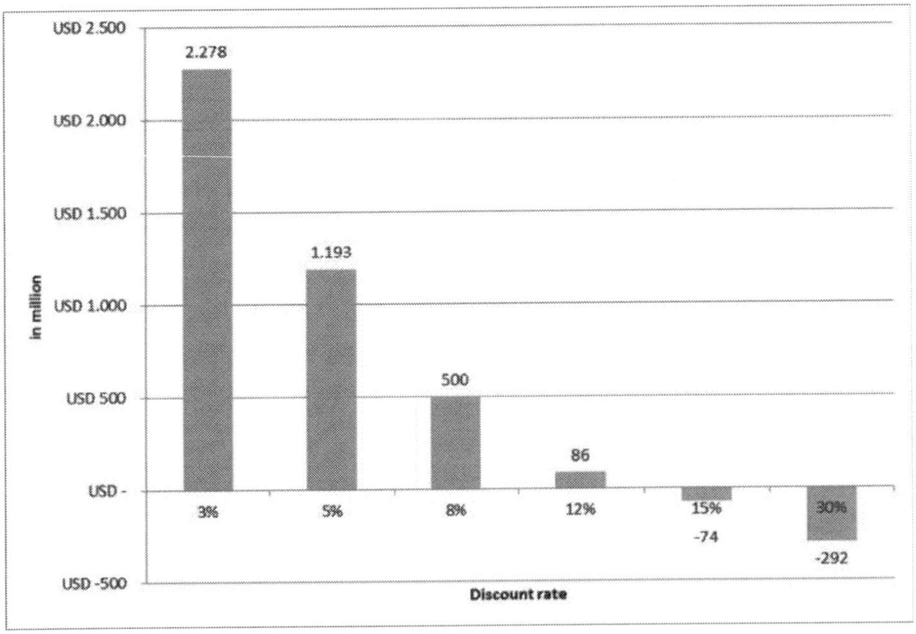

Instead of using a discount rate that is based on e.g. weighted average cost of capital (WACC), RADR uses a risk-adjusted rate:

$$NPVradr = \sum_{t=0}^{n} \frac{Ct}{(1+r)t}$$

where:
r = Rf + Rb + Rp and Rf + Rb = d
Rf = risk-free rate
Rb = adjustment for normal business risk
Rp = adjustment for the risk of a specific project.

In the CE method, a risk-free discount rate is used, but risky future cash flows are connected to certainty equivalent cash flows:

$$NPVce = \sum_{t=0}^{n} \frac{Ct.\alpha t}{(1+d)^{t}}$$

where:
Ct = the expected net cash flow in period t
αt = the CE factor associated with the risk in year t (e.g. $\alpha 1$ = 0.7 means a 70 percent probability of getting C1 in year 1).

A somewhat more complicated approach is to cope with uncertainty using the sensitivity analyses method, sometimes known as the scenario analyses method. This method examines how the NPV or IRR changes relate to the assumptions made. Three sets of assumptions are considered: based on a worst-case scenario, based on a best-case scenario, and based on a scenario that most probably can be expected. The expected NPV (eNPV) is defined as:

eNPV = (NPV w × probability w) + (NPV e × probability e)
+ (NPV b × probability b)

where:
NPV w = NPV for the worst-case scenario
NPV e = NPV for the most probable scenario
NPV b = NPV for the best-case scenario
Σ probabilities = 1.

There are also very sophisticated risk-adjusted DCF methods such as Monte Carlo simulations, decision tree analysis (DTA), etc. Monte Carlo is a simulation technique in which the NPV calculation goes through multiple iterations using a different input value (sales expectations, costs, probabilities) every time, the end result being a frequency distribution of NPVs. The real role of such simulations is to understand the way in which the values vary with the parameters of the model constructed.

DTA allows for more flexibility, as in each branch an underlying DCF analysis is done, starting with the final ones and working backwards in time to give a present value. DTA is a decision support tool that uses a tree-like graphic of decisions and the possible consequences, including probability of the outcomes, related resources and costs, and expected values for each branch (Smith and Nau, 1995).

Option pricing theory methods (Copeland and Antikaron, 2001), such as the continuous-time Black-Scholes option pricing models (Chriss, 1997), account for the changing risk of future cash flows. The present value of returns the company will receive from the investment is linked to the value of the shares subject to the call option. Several authors promote the application of option-based valuation methods in strategic investments rather than DCF models only, and have developed multiple-scenario integrated models complementing DCF and option pricing techniques, but these are complicated and not part of this introductory course.

The discount rate "d"

As shown in Figure 6.8, the percentage used for the discount rate can have a significant impact on the intrinsic value of a project (NPV). Which percentage should be used? There are three important aspects that need to be taken in account:

- inflation
- alternative rates of return for investments
- the risks associated with the project – technological, scientific, and economic.

Inflation

During the last decades all countries around the world have experienced inflation, and unfortunately this will not change in the future. The measure commonly used is known as the Consumer Prices Index; economists often use the gross domestic product deflator as an alternative measure. The US inflation rate in 2010 was 1.63 percent and in the

European Union 1.91 percent (www.forecast-chart.com or www.global-rates.com), but average inflation in 2010 was quite low compared to previous years. In general, it is appropriate to use 3 percent as an average of the inflation rate.

Our previous example of the net monthly salary of €2,500 noted that ten years from now this amount would be worth less. Due to inflation, today's value would be:

$$€2{,}500 / (1 + 3\%)^{10} = €1{,}860$$

Hence if our investments are to yield more than the loss of money due to inflation, the discount rate needs to be higher than the inflation rate.

Risk-free investments

In some countries government stocks, securities, or bonds are available with a guaranteed fixed rate of return, e.g. US Treasury bills, notes, or bonds. A ten-year US Treasury note issued in February 2011 guaranteed an interest rate of 3.63 percent (www.treasurydirect.gov). In Belgium a *staatsbon* of February 2011 for a term of eight years guaranteed annual interest of 3.75 percent. In this example, if you buy a 2011 *staatsbon* for €2,500, after eight years you will receive, guaranteed:

$$€2{,}500 \times (1.0375)^{8} = €3{,}356$$

Hence the discount rate used should be higher than any risk-free guaranteed interest rate. If it is lower than this, one would be better off investing in e.g. the Belgian *staatsbon.*

Corporate cost of capital

Enterprises are legal entities that require money to work with, and they can acquire this from banks/debt, equity investors, etc. The company needs to consider the total rate of return it must pay to its investors – who rightly expect a higher rate of return because they own less secure rights in comparison to a holder of a bond with guaranteed interest. Thus a corporation's weighted average cost of capital is normally higher than its debt. The calculation of WACCs is quite complicated and requires model-based calculations, but fortunately they are often published (see, for example, www.wikiwealth.com and Pages.stern.nyu.edu). Some of the WACCs for life sciences in January 2011 are presented in Table 6.15.

Table 6.15 WACC values for various industries, 2011

Industry	Cost of capital (%)
Beverages	7.45
Biotechnology	8.61
Drugs	8.59
Food processing	6.76
Toiletries/cosmetics	8.68
Water utility	4.89

Corporate return on capital

Every enterprise aims to provide a return on capital that exceeds its cost of capital (WACC). Hence a company will select projects, mergers, acquisitions, and licensing deals that will earn a return on capital that exceeds the company's WACC. Return on equity (ROE) is calculated by dividing the earnings for a period by the average shareholders' equity during that period. ROE data are readily available for each public company. Of course, ROE can vary over time and can be significantly affected by e.g. an economic downturn. For Pfizer the ROE at the beginning of 2011 was 7 percent, which was the same as its WACC. For J&J it was 8 percent, just 1 percent higher than its WACC of 7 percent. Normally companies try to achieve double-digit ROEs, and 12–15 percent is quite common. Companies have a lot of products and/or projects, which helps spreading the risk. To evaluate one particular investment, be it in R&D projects or an in-licensing opportunity, the company expects an additional return premium due to the risk associated with any single investment.

Venture capital

Venture capitalists (VCs) are another category of technology investors. They often invest in young or start-up companies, which receive this venture capital in "funds" from a set of wealthy investors. VC companies which are too optimistic in evaluating new opportunities quickly face the fact that they can provide very low returns on investments, hence they will have significant problems finding additional funds in a second round of investments. Young or start-up companies often promote a very optimistic 20 or even 50 percent return on investments, in order to attract sufficient investors or VCs. Start-up companies can represent a high risk due to new technology, but also due to their management having little business experience.

Determining "d"

As we have seen, there are various angles in looking at the discount rate. It needs to take in account inflation, cost of capital, and expected return, but it should also be linked to the technological and economic risk associated with the product/technology. Thus we could define the discount rate as follows:

d = corporate baseline + number associated with technological risk
+ number associated with economic risk

By doing this, we automatically move into risk-adjusted DCF methods such as RADR (see above).

The scoring system explained earlier in this chapter can be helpful in determining the risk-associated numbers. Another approach could be the classification concept. Based on experience, people have established/defined different categories of opportunities in relation to the associated risk and allocated a specific discount rate window to the different categories. One classification, as defined by Razgaitis (2009), is presented in Table 6.16. A classification approach can also be enhanced by coupling it to the scoring system.

In our previous example of OCAL-1 for the treatment of ocular allergy we use 8 percent as a discount rate, which is equal to the ROE for several pharmaceutical companies in early 2011. As noted, OCAL-1 is in an early phase of development, with a high risk in eventually commercializing the product. If we use a discount rate of e.g. 30 percent to cover this high risk, the calculated NPV is –US$239.5 million, i.e. highly negative and not worth doing. Via the "Goal Seek" function in Excel we can calculate the annual sales needed to have an NPV of zero as a minimum: US$1,249 million (for a discount rate of 30 percent). For this reason large pharmacy companies are (currently) not interested in early-phase products with "rather low" sales potential.

One can investigate how sales could be increased, e.g. by expanding into new territories or markets. In our case of OCAL-1, for instance, prescription drugs represent only 10 percent of the ocular allergy market. The majority of patients (90 percent) buy their treatments over the counter (OTC), so we could increase the sales of OCAL-1 by getting approval to sell it OTC.

Table 6.16 **Classes of opportunities with different levels of risk and related discount rates**

Class	Characterization of opportunity	Example	Discount rate window
0	Risk free	Expression of a production line for an already commercialized product	8–18%
I	Very low risk	Incremental improvements on an established product	15–20%
II	Low risk	Making a product with new features for known customers, using known technology	20–30%
III	Moderate risk	Making a new product for a known customer segment using well-understood technology	25–35%
IV	High risk	Making a new product via not well-understood technology and/or marketing it to a new segment	30–40%
V	Very high risk	Making a new product with new technology for a new customer segment/market	35–45%
VI	Extremely high risk	Creating a start-up company to go into business making a product not presently sold using unproven technologies	50% or higher

Source: Razgaitis (2009).

Another approach to bring the NPV into positive numbers (Figure 6.9) is to work on the related costings, e.g. reduce the clinical trial costs by organizing trials in lower-cost countries, do the trials more efficiently, use existing infrastructure and equipment for production of the new product/technology, etc. Hence studying all the different parameters and their effect on NPV is highly recommended. Excel models make this quite easy using functions such as "Goal Seek" and "Scenario Manager".

Dividing the intrinsic value

Let us now look at how the intrinsic value of the new IP can be divided between the licensor (the seller) and the licensee (the buyer). There are two main concepts.

Figure 6.9 Factors to improve the value of a project

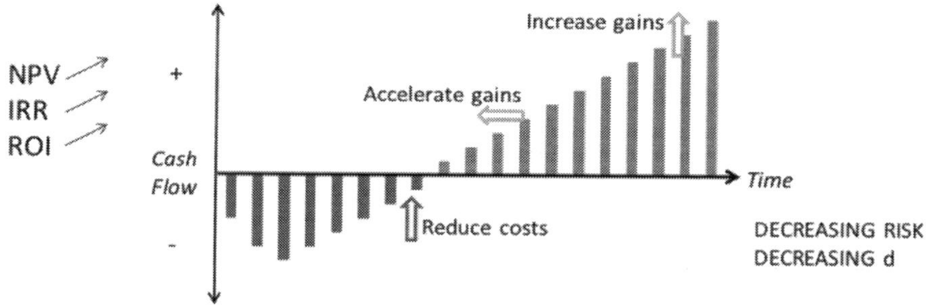

Excess earnings concept

If a licensee uses a DCF method where both the expected ROI and the risk related to the project are incorporated, then all the "positive value" of the calculated NPV must go to the licensor. How this remaining positive value is paid to the licensor depends on the agreement:

- the licensee buys the patent and pays a lump sum equal to the NPV
- the remaining NPV is spread via upfront payments, stage payments, and royalties.

Excel allows easy creation of models that can incorporate these factors and related values. With the "Goal Seek" function it is possible to adjust these values in such a way that the NPV is set to zero (and the original positive NPV flows to the licensor).

The 25 percent rule

If seller and buyer agree that a DCF method will be used that provides only the appropriate present values of all the future benefits, given the risk of the project, the resulting NPV should be divided in a way that reflects the contribution (investments, IP, etc.) of each party. A good way to do this is using the 25 percent rule presented earlier, i.e. 25 percent of the resulting NPV is retained by the licensor and 75 percent of the value goes to the licensee. This 25 percent of the NPV can be paid as a lump sum or spread over time via upfront, stage, and royalty payments (Figure 6.10).

Figure 6.10 Distribution of the intrinsic value based on the 25 percent rule of thumb

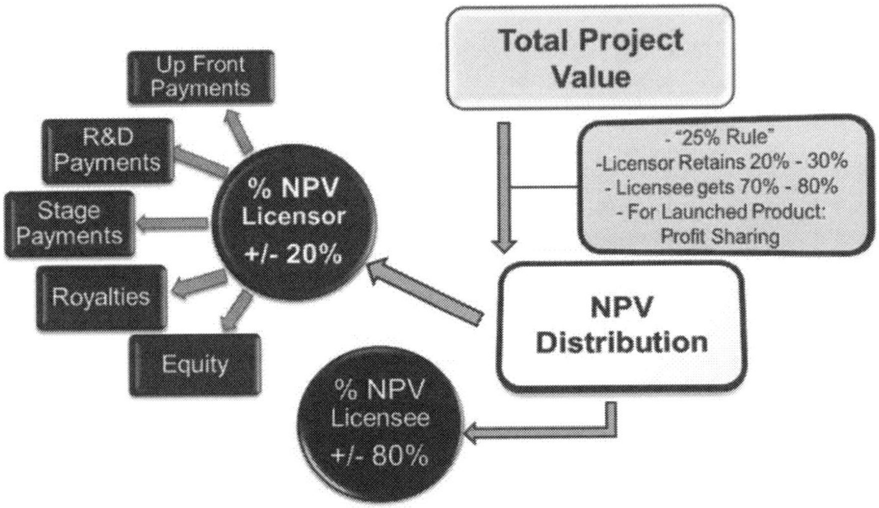

For fully developed products or technology, ready to be launched, the distribution of the intrinsic value (NPV) will be more towards split profit.

Let us illustrate the value distribution between licensor and licensee with another example. In 2007 a group at Ghent University started researching alternatives to antibiotic growth promoters (AGPs) in feed, since these AGPs were banned by law in the European Union in 2006. In 2008 the research group took a patent on POLYBUT-1, a polymer of a short-chain fatty acid for use in feed. By 2009 it had spent US$240,000 on basic research and the patent cost was estimated to be US$85,000. In 2010 the research group moved into negotiations with a worldwide feed additive producer. The licensee would develop the product, register it in major markets, and commercialize it worldwide under an exclusive license agreement.

Marketing had shown that in 2010 maximum annual sales of such a product could be US$15 million, and the annual growth rate was estimated to be approximately 6 percent. But the scientific community was working on the development of large numbers of competitor products and technologies, so the product lifespan was estimated to last until 2020, with several competitors entering the market in 2017, causing a decrease in sales/market share of 30 percent.

The COGS in general for the feed additive industry is approximately 45 percent of net sales, and the total expenses for overheads, sales, marketing, etc. are approximately 48 percent of net sales. A clear proof of concept was established during basic research and large-scale production of POLYBUT-1 was available. Hence the risk was rather low, so a discount rate of 12 percent was used. The calculation of the intrinsic value is presented in Figure 6.11.

The project has a total positive value of US$4.13 million and an IRR of 65 percent. How to distribute this value between licensor and licensee? The model in Excel can be expanded to an NPV for the licensor, based on royalties received minus expenses/costs carried, and one for the licensee, based on sales minus royalties paid and expenses/costs carried. The upfront and stage payments could be based on the previously mentioned rule of thumb, i.e. taking 10 percent of the retained intrinsic value. In this example, however, the upfront payment is based on the patent cost plus 20 percent make-up. The reason is the related industrial sector: agricultural feed is a high-volume, low-margin business, making it difficult to negotiate high upfront or stage payments. An annual R&D fee until product launch was incorporated to ensure the licensee would work promptly on product development to get it registered and launched as soon as possible. The remaining related value for the licensor would be paid as royalties on net sales. With the "Goal Seek" function the royalty rate could easily be determined in the generated model to be 1.5 percent on net sales.

As shown in Figure 6.11, the value retained by the licensor was approximately 25 percent and the licensee received 75 percent of the intrinsic value. The final agreement included articles on minimum royalties, which were set at the royalties received after the first year of sales, annually increased based on the Consumer Prices Index. In addition, articles regarding termination were included, e.g. launching the product a maximum of three years after signing the agreement, and after termination all rights would return to the licensor.

In a similar way, we can look at the FRAND approach. In our POLYBUT-1 example the licensor invested $240,000 in research and $85,000 in patent costs. The licensee invested $400,000 in total. According to FRAND the licensor should receive:

$$\$325{,}000 \,/\, \$725{,}000 \times \$4{,}132{,}927 \text{ (project NPV)} = \$1{,}852{,}691$$

The $1,852,691 project value can then be distributed in stage payments and royalties on net sales. The licensor receives 44.83 percent of the

Figure 6.11 NPV calculation of POLYBUT-1 example and distribution between licensor and licensee

POLYBUT-1 as a AGP replacer in feed

SALES			
Top Annual Sales	$15.000.000	Duration of top sales	4
Estimated annual growth rate	6%	Afterwards yearly decrease	30%
Product Launch in year	2011	Expected life time till year	2020
Penetration till top sales		Patent filed in year	2008
1 year after launch	5%		
2 year after launch	20%		
3 year after launch	40%		
4 year after launch	75%		

COST	
Basic research (licensor)/year	$120.000
Development (licensee)/year	$200.000
Patent costs	$85.000
COGS as a % of sales	45%
Total expenses as a % of sales	48%
discount rate	12%

INTRINSIC VALUE	2008	2009	2010	2011	2012	2013	2014	2015	2016	2017	2018	2019	2020
Sales potential	$0	$0	$15.000.000	$15.900.000	$16.854.000	$17.865.240	$18.937.154	$20.073.384	$21.277.787	$22.554.454	$23.907.721	$25.342.184	$26.862.715
Sales	$0	$0	$0	$795.000	$3.370.800	$7.146.096	$14.202.866	$20.073.384	$21.277.787	$22.554.454	$16.735.405	$17.739.529	$18.803.901
Basic research	$120.000	$120.000	$0	$0	$0	$0	$0	$0	$0	$0	$0	$0	$0
Development	$0	$0	$200.000	$200.000	$0	$0	$0	$0	$0	$0	$0	$0	$0
Patent cost	$0	$85.000	$0	$0	$0	$0	$0	$0	$0	$0	$0	$0	$0
COGS	$0	$0	$0	$357.750	$1.516.860	$3.215.743	$6.391.290	$9.033.023	$9.575.004	$10.149.504	$7.530.932	$7.982.788	$8.461.755
Total Expenses (sales, marketing etc.)	$0	$0	$0	$381.600	$1.617.984	$3.430.126	$6.817.376	$9.635.224	$10.213.338	$10.826.138	$8.032.994	$8.514.974	$9.025.872
Net Cash	-$120.000	-$205.000	-$200.000	-$144.350	$235.956	$500.227	$994.201	$1.405.137	$1.489.445	$1.578.812	$1.171.478	$1.241.767	$1.316.273
Discounted Net Cash	-$120.000	-$205.000	-$200.000	-$128.884	$188.103	$356.051	$631.832	$797.312	$754.599	$714.174	$473.140	$447.794	$423.805
Accumulated Net Cash	-$120.000	-$325.000	-$525.000	-$653.884	-$465.781	-$109.730	$522.103	$1.319.415	$2.074.014	$2.788.189	$3.261.329	$3.709.123	$4.132.927
PROJECT NPV	$4.132.927												
PROJECT IRR	65%												

ROYALTIES	2008	2009	2010	2011	2012	2013	2014	2015	2016	2017	2018	2019	2020
Upfront (patent cost +20%)			$102.000										
R&D Fee (annual fee till launch)			65000	65000									
Stage Payments after first sales					150000								
Royalties as a % on net sales	1,5%			11.925	50.562	107.191	213.043	301.101	319.167	338.317	251.031	266.093	282.059
TOTAL			$167.000	$76.925	$200.562	$107.191	$213.043	$301.101	$319.167	$338.317	$251.031	$266.093	$282.059

LICENSEE	2008	2009	2010	2011	2012	2013	2014	2015	2016	2017	2018	2019	2020
Sales	$0	$0	$0	$795.000	$3.370.800	$7.146.096	$14.202.866	$20.073.384	$21.277.787	$22.554.454	$16.735.405	$17.739.529	$18.803.901
Development cost	$0	$0	$200.000	$200.000	$0	$0	$0	$0	$0	$0	$0	$0	$0
COGS	$0	$0	$0	$357.750	$1.516.860	$3.215.743	$6.391.290	$9.033.023	$9.575.004	$10.149.504	$7.530.932	$7.982.788	$8.461.755
Total Expenses (sales, marketing etc.)	$0	$0	$0	$381.600	$1.617.984	$3.430.126	$6.817.376	$9.635.224	$10.213.338	$10.826.138	$8.032.994	$8.514.974	$9.025.872
Royalties to Licensor	$0	$0	$167.000	$76.925	$200.562	$107.191	$213.043	$301.101	$319.167	$338.317	$251.031	$266.093	$282.059
Net Cash	$0	$0	-$367.000	-$221.275	$35.394	$393.035	$781.158	$1.104.036	$1.170.278	$1.240.495	$920.447	$975.674	$1.034.215
Discounted Net Cash	$0	$0	-$367.000	-$197.567	$28.216	$279.755	$496.440	$626.460	$592.899	$561.137	$371.753	$351.838	$332.989
Accumulated Net Cash	$0	$0	-$367.000	-$564.567	-$536.351	-$256.596	$239.843	$866.303	$1.459.203	$2.020.340	$2.392.093	$2.743.931	$3.076.920
NPV Licensee	$3.076.920	As a % of the total project NPV			74,45%								

LICENSOR	2008	2009	2010	2011	2012	2013	2014	2015	2016	2017	2018	2019	2020
Royalties received from Licensee	$0	$0	$167.000	$76.925	$200.562	$107.191	$213.043	$301.101	$319.167	$338.317	$251.031	$266.093	$282.059
Basic Research	$120.000	$120.000	$0	$0	$0	$0	$0	$0	$0	$0	$0	$0	$0
Patent cost	$0	$85.000	$0	$0	$0	$0	$0	$0	$0	$0	$0	$0	$0
Net Cash	-$120.000	-$205.000	$167.000	$76.925	$200.562	$107.191	$213.043	$301.101	$319.167	$338.317	$251.031	$266.093	$282.059
Discounted Net Cash	-$120.000	-$205.000	$167.000	$68.683	$159.887	$76.297	$135.393	$170.853	$161.700	$153.037	$101.387	$95.956	$90.815
Accumulated Net Cash	-$120.000	-$325.000	-$158.000	-$89.317	$70.570	$146.867	$282.259	$453.112	$614.812	$767.849	$869.236	$965.192	$1.056.007
NPV Licensor	$1.056.007	As a % of the total project NPV			25,55%								

project value, versus 25 percent using the 25 percent rule, thus the FRAND rate is rather high in this case.

Identifying possible licensees, negotiating terms and conditions, and drafting the legal agreement are not part of this introduction to valorization, but some general aspects can be shared. When identifying and shortlisting possible companies as licensee candidates, it is important to evaluate them on pre-set criteria, such as:

- experience in the related business sector
- presence in the different regions of the world
- market share in the different regions
- operational activities and infrastructure
- sales and marketing force in the different regions
- product portfolio (is there a competitor product to your new IP?)
- R&D pipeline
- R&D capabilities (e.g. to develop the licensed technology further)
- cost structure and financials
- company culture and vision.

When moving into negotiations, after a due diligence it is important to work towards a win-win situation. The models and concepts presented in previous sections can be good tools for this. After an agreement has been reached, a legal contract needs to be generated and signed. Such a contract typically includes:

- names and addresses of the parties
- effective date
- subject (product/technology) and related references to the IP (e.g. patents)
- type of agreement, e.g. exclusive license, co-marketing, etc.
- territory, e.g. worldwide or United States, or excluding European Union, etc.
- activities and related cost for each party (product development, sales, production)
- royalty payments
- articles regarding termination and duration

- warranties
- articles on confidentiality
- governing law
- signatures of legal representatives of the parties.

Valorization via a new company

Besides licensing the new IP to an established company in return for royalties, it is also possible to set up a new company that will commercialize the new IP. This can be a spin-off company, or a joint venture between two or more companies, etc.

The concepts and DCF models can be part of the business plan for the new company. It requires much more preparation and details in comparison to out-licensing. The *pro forma* that needs to be generated should mainly be based on bottom-up-derived data, e.g. determination of selling price, detailed costing for production, assessment of the market segment, number of customers, number of competitors, market trends and dynamics, etc.

How to generate business plans and build new companies is not part of this book. Nevertheless, it is important to consider IP-related issues when setting up new companies.

The Rolling Stones established approximately 30 years ago a company in Holland that owns the copyrights to all their songs, name, etc. The main reason for this is that in Holland income from royalties is only taxed at 1.5 percent compared to 40 percent in the UK. This way the band (Mick Jagger, Charlie Watts, and Keith Richards, but not Ron Wood) only paid US$7.2 million in taxes over the past 20 years on earnings over US$450 million.

When Ireland announced in 2006 that it would sharply curtail a tax break regarding royalties, U2 became sophisticated about finding overseas shelters for its money and also moved to Holland. The Dutch shelter is simple: royalty-based income is exempt from taxes. Although the base corporate tax rate in the Netherlands is approximately 30 percent, the domestic tax rate on royalties brings that rate down substantially. Furthermore, it is not required to have actual running operations in a Dutch holding company. Tax shelters in the Netherlands are not only used by artists, but also by large (production) companies such as Coca-Cola, Sun Microsystems, Nike, and Ikea.

Since 1982 the Ikea group has been controlled by a non-profit entity called Stichting Ingka Foundation. This foundation controls Ingka Holding BV, another company in Holland that holds the rights of trade names (e.g. Ikea) and copyrights to all designs and other IP. All the Ikea companies around the globe must pay royalties to use the name Ikea, sell Ikea designs, etc. For instance, more than 250 Ikea stores worldwide pay 3 percent of their annual turnover to use the "Ikea concept".

The Ikea empire had a turnover of €21.2 billion in 2007. The profit of the Dutch holding can be paid as a dividend to the shareholders. Shareholders need to pay taxes on this dividend, conforming to the tax legislation of the country they live in or of their citizenship. (Some countries such as Monaco have zero tax on income from dividends.) This contributed to the fact that Ingvar Kamprad, founder of Ikea, who currently lives in Switzerland, was worth US$31 billion net in 2008 according to *Forbes* (2008), making him the seventh-richest person in the world.

The fact that in some countries no (or reduced) taxes need to be paid on income generated from royalties or sales of IP-based matter can also be a good argument in license negotiations. By obtaining a license on an IP-protected product, a licensee could achieve a good turnover on which less corporate tax needs to be paid (depending on the country); savings made due to reduced corporate taxes can help make the payment of royalties more attractive. These systems have creative names such as "double Irish arrangements" and "Dutch sandwiches".

Notes

1. *Innogenetics N.V. versus Abbott Lab.*, Fed. Cir. 2008.
2. *Georgia-Pacific Corp. v. United States Plywood Corp.*, 318 F. Supp. 1116, 1119-20 (S.D.N.Y. 1970), modified and aff'd, 446 F.2d 295 (2d Cir.); *Unisplay, S.A. v. American Electronic Sign Co., Inc.*, 69 F.3d 512, 517 n.7 (Fed. Cir. 1995).
3. *Uniloc USA versus Microsoft*, U.S. CAFC, 2010-10 35, -105, 4 January 2011.

References and further reading

References

AIPLA (2005) *Report of the Economic Survey 2005*. Arlington, VA: American Intellectual Property Law Association.

AIPLA (2011) *Report of the Economic Survey 2011*. Arlington, VA: American Intellectual Property Law Association.

Arnold, T. and Headley, T. (1987) "Factors in pricing licenses", *Les Nouvelles*, March: 19–22.

Baggott, S., Germeraad, P., Khan, R., Oliver, W., Peregrim, J., and Wandji, S.-A. (2008) "Licensing's key role in global innovation", *Les Nouvelles*, December: 261–71.

Baker, H.K. and English, P. (2011) *Capital Budgeting Valuation: Financial Analysis for Today's Investment Projects*. Hoboken, NJ: John Wiley & Sons.

Bouckley, B. (2011) "Goldenfry Foods wins trade secrets case", FoodManufacture, 1 March; available at: *www.foodmanufacture.co.uk/Business-News/Goldenfry-Foods-wins-trade-secrets-case* (accessed: 6 January 2012).

Chriss, N.A. (1997) *The Black-Scholes and Beyond Option Pricing Models*. New York: McGraw-Hill.

Copeland, T. and Antikaron, V. (2001) *Real Options: A Practitioners Guide*. New York: Texere Publishing.

de Vuyst, B. (2006) *Handboek Octrooien*. Bruges: die Keure.

DiMasi, J., Hansen, R.H., and Grabowski, H.G. (2003) "The price of innovation: new estimates of drug development costs", *Journal of Health Economics*, 22: 151–85.

EPO (2008) "Agreement on the application of Article 65 EPC – London Agreement", 30 April; available at: *www.epo.org/law-practice/legal-texts/london-agreement.html* (accessed: 9 July 2014).

European Commission (2007) "Fact sheet: European policy for quality of agricultural products".

European Commission (2010) "PDO and PGI agricultural products", newsletter, Agricultural and Rural Development; available at: *http://ec.europa.eu/agriculture/quality/schemes/newsletter-2010_en.pdf* (accessed: 12 January 2012).

European Commission (2012) "What ACTA is about"; available at: *http://trade.ec.europa.eu/doclib/docs/2012/january/tradoc_149003.pdf* (accessed: 14 July 2014).

FindLaw (undated) "Innogenetics v. Abbott Laboratories"; available at: *http://caselaw.findlaw.com/us-federal-circuit/1063919.html* (accessed: 17 July 2014).

Forbes (2007) "In pictures: the richest 20 women in entertainment"; available at: *www.forbes.com/2007/01/17/richest-women-entertainment-tech-media-cz_lg_richwomen07_0118womenstars_slide_3.html* (accessed: 12 December 2011).

Forbes (2008) "The world's billionaires: No. 7 Ingvar Kamprad & family", 3 May; available at: *www.forbes.com/lists/2008/10/billionaires08_Ingvar-Kamprad-family_BWQ7.html* (accessed: 10 May 2008).

Goldscheider, R., Jarosz, J., and Mulhern, C. (2002) "Use of the 25 per cent rule in valuing IP", *Les Nouvelles*, December: 123–33.

Grabowski, H., Vernon, J., and DiMasi, J.A. (2002) "Returns on research and development for 1990s new drug introductions", *PharmacoEconomics*, 20(3): 11–29.

Granstrand, O. and Holgersson, M. (2012) "The 25 per cent rule revisited and a new investment-based method for determining FRAND licensing royalties", *Les Nouvelles*, September: 188–95.

Hart, T. (2012) "Rehabilitating Locke: the labor justification of copyright", Copyhype, 5 March; available at: *www.copyhype.com/2012/03/rehabilitating-locke-the-labor-justification-of-copyright/* (accessed: 12 February 2013).

Hillier, D., Ross, S., Westerfield, R., Jaffe, J., and Jordan, B. (2010) *Corporate Finance, European Edition*. New York: McGraw-Hill Education.

Interbrand (2012) "Press release"; available at: *www.interbrand.com/en/news-room/press-releases/2012-10-02-7543da7.aspx* (accessed: 7 June 2013).

International Trademark Association (undated) "Madrid Agreement and Protocol – a practitioners guide"; available at: *www.inta.org/MadridProtocol/Pages/MadridProtocol.aspx* (accessed: 14 November 2013).

Jarczyk, D. (2011) "Replacing the 25 per cent rule with fact-based evidence – a guide to finding and analyzing royalty rates", *Les Nouvelles*, December: 179–82.

Kidder, D.G. and O'Brien, V.E. (2011) "Simply wrong: the 25 per cent rule examined", *Les Nouvelles*, December: 163–8.

Lu, J. (2011) "The 25 per cent rule still rules: new evidence from pro forma analysis in royalty rates", *Les Nouvelles*, March: 14–17.

Mathieu, M.P. (2008) *Parexel's Bio/Pharmaceutical R&D Statistical Sourcebook 2007/2008*. Waltham, MA: Parexel International Corporation.

OECD (2009) *OECD Science, Technology and Industry Scoreboard 2009*. Paris: OECD.

OECD (2010) *Measuring Innovation*. Paris: OECD.

OHIM (2014) "European Trade Mark and Design Network"; available at: *www.tmdn.org/tmdsview-web/welcome* (accessed: 9 July 2014).

Porter, M., Mills, R., and Weinstein, R. (2008) "Industry norms and reasonable royalty rate determination", *Les Nouvelles*, March: 47–64.

Razgaitis, R. (2009) *Valuation and Dealmaking of Technology-based Intellectual Property*. Hoboken, NJ: John Wiley & Sons.

Roland Berger Market Research (2004) "Study on the cost of patenting", August; available at: *www.effi.org/system/files?file=cost_anaylsis_2005_study_en.pdf* (accessed: 9 July 2014).

Rose, M. (1988) "The author as proprietor: *Donaldson v. Becket* and the genealogy of modern authorship", *Representations*, 23: 51–85.

Scott, D. (2005) *Pharmaceutical Licensing*, SCRIP Written Courses 3. London: T&F Informa.

Seget, S. (2006) "Pharmaceutical licensing strategies. Best practices in deal-making, valuations and strategic management", management report, Business Insights, London.

Smith, J.E. and Nau, R.F. (1995) "Valuing risky projects: option pricing and decision analysis", *Management Science*, 41: 795–816.

The Guardian (2011) "James Patterson brand makes him world's best-paid writer", 18 August; available at: *www.theguardian.com/books/2011/aug/18/publishing-jkrowling* (accessed: 25 May 2012).

Trading Economics (2010) "Euro area inflation rate"; available at: *www.tradingeconomics.com/euro-area/inflation-cpi* (accessed: 8 April 2011).

Tuckness, A. (2012) "Locke's political philosophy", *Stanford Encyclopedia of Philosophy*, Winter; available at: *http://plato.stanford.edu/archives/win2012/entries/locke-political/* (accessed: 12 February 2013).

USLegal.com (undated) "Prior art law & legal definition"; available at: *http://definitions.uslegal.com/p/prior-art/* (accessed: 15 May 2014).

Van Bree, I., De Meulenaer, B., Samapundo, S., Vermeulen, A., Ragaert, P., Meas, K.C., De Baets, B., and Devlieghere, F. (2010) "Predicting the headspace oxygen level due to oxygen permeation across multilayer polymer packaging materials: a practical software simulation tool", *Innovative Food Science and Emerging Technologies*, 11: 511–19.

Wikileaks (2008) "Proposed US ACTA plurilateral intellectual property trade agreement (2007)", 22 March; available at: *http://wikileaks.org/wiki/Proposed_US_ACTA_multi-lateral_intellectual_property_trade_agreement_%282007%29* (accessed: 14 July 2014).

Further reading

Bloom, M. (2003) *AUTM Technology Transfer Practice Manual*, 2nd edn. Deerfield, IL: Association of University Technology Managers.

de Vuyst, B. (2009) *Handboek Tekeningen en Modellen*. Bruges: die Keure Business & Economics.

de Vuyst, B. (2010) *Handboek Databanken*. Bruges: die Keure Business & Economics.

Dodgson, M., Gann, D., and Salter, A. (2008) *The Management of Technological Innovation*. New York: Oxford University Press.

Folon, J. (2010) *Auteursrecht en intellectuele eigendom: vragen en antwoorden, gids voor de federale communicatoren*. Brussels: Leroy.

Goldscheider, R. (2002) *The LESI Guide to Licensing Best Practices: Strategic Issues and Contemporary Realities*. Hoboken, NJ: John Wiley & Sons.

Gravez, B. (2007) *Ons Patent Boekje, Een handige gids voor kmo-bedrijfsleiders over intellectuele eigendom*. Brussels: Instituut voor Innovatie door Wetenschap en Technologie.

Luenberger, D.G. (1998) *Investment Science*. New York: Oxford University Press.

O'Donnell, R.W., O'Malley, J.J., Huis, R.J., and Halt, G.B. (2008) *Intellectual Property in the Food Technology Industry: Protecting Your Innovation*. New York: Springer Science+Business Media.

Parr, R.L. and Smith, G.V. (2005) *Intellectual Property: Valuation, Exploitation, and Infringement Damages*. Hoboken, NJ: John Wiley & Sons.

Useful websites

Agreement on Trade-Related Aspects of Intellectual Property Rights (TRIPS)	www.wto.org/english/docs_e/27_trips.pdf
Benelux Office for Intellectual Property	www.boip.int
Community Plant Variety Office (CPVO)	www.CPVR.info
European Patent Office (EPO)	www.epo.org
EPO forms and fees	www.epo.org/applying/forms-fees.html
Güfa	www.guefa.de
Internet Corporation for Assigned Names and Numbers (ICANN)	icann.org
Office for Harmonization of the Internal Market (OHIM)	Oami.europa.eu
SABAM	www.sabam.be
Securities and Exchange Commission (SEC)	www.SEC.gov
US Copyright Office	www.copyright.gov
US Patent and Trademark Office (USPTO)	www.uspto.gov
World Intellectual Property Organization (WIPO)	www.wipo.int
World Trade Organization (WTO)	www.wto.org

Appendix 1
An example of a CDA

CONFIDENTIALITY AND NON-DISCLOSURE AGREEMENT

This Agreement is made on this <DAY>, <MONTH>, <YEAR> ("Effective Date") between

<COMPANY NAME A>

Address

(Hereinafter referred to as "<Company Name A>")

And

<COMPANY NAME B>

Address

(Hereinafter referred to as "<Company Name B>")

Hereinafter individually referred to as the "Party" and collectively as the "Parties"

WHEREAS, <Company Name> is engaged in the business etc.

WHEREAS, <Company Name> is engaged in the business etc.

WHEREAS, the parties are in the process of discussing potential etc.

WHEREAS, the parties acknowledge that their discussions might lead to some form etc.

WHEREAS, the parties desire to protect the confidentiality of certain information either may disclose to the other party through this agreement.

THEREFORE, in consideration of mutual promises and other valuable information exchanged and intended to be legally bound, the parties hereby agree and contract as follows.

1. DEFINITIONS

1.1 "Affiliates" means with respect to each party, the legal entities that control, are controlled by, or are under common control with such party.

1.2 "Confidential Information" shall be deemed to include information on <SUBJECT> and includes (a) the following types of information, whether or not so declared in writing: discoveries, techniques, know-how, ideas, concepts, formulations, molecules, structures, drug delivery regimes, designs, drawings, specifications, techniques, models, prototypes, data, source code, object code, documentation, manuals, diagrams, flow charts, schematics, research, process, procedures, functions, and all analyses, compilations, forecasts, studies or other documents, marketing techniques and materials, marketing and development plans, customer names and other information related to customer price lists, pricing policies and financial information, any and all related materials, inventions, practices, methods, knowledge, skill experience, test data, analytical and quality control data and manufacturing and patent data or descriptions; (b) any similar information disclosed to the Receiving Party or its employees prior to the execution of this Agreement; (c) any material transfer from the Disclosing Party to the Receiving Party along with the relevant proprietary information.

The term "Confidential Information" shall include any and all information and other materials disclosed, furnished, communicated, perceived or supplied by one party to the other party or by virtue of the one party visiting, witnessing and/or observing the facilities, laboratories or factory of the other party and/or its affiliate companies or associates could be reasonably assumed to be Confidential Information. Any information disclosed on <SUBJECT> by one party will be considered Confidential Information of the party by the other party whether or not such information is designated as "Confidential" or "Proprietary", or identified during the course of an oral disclosure as confidential.

1.3 "Disclosing Party" means the party or its employees that disclose Confidential Information to the other party (Recipient).

1.4 Disclosure Period" means the period during which either party may be disclosing Confidential Information to the other party. The Disclosure Period shall commence from the effective date set forth above, and shall expire <NUMBER> year(s) after such date, unless terminated earlier in writing by mutual agreement of the parties or upon the request of either party in writing.

1.5 "Recipient" means the party or its employees who receive Confidential Information from the other party (Disclosing Party).

1.6 "Exempt Information" means information that the Recipient can demonstrate by written records (a) was in its possession prior to the time of disclosure; (b) is or becomes public knowledge through no fault, omission, or other act of the Receiving Party; (c) is obtained from a third party under no obligation of confidentiality to the Disclosing Party; or (d) was independently developed by or for the Recipient without violating the terms of this Agreement.

1.7 "Permitted User" means an individual who (1) (a) is the Recipient's director, officer, consultant, financial advisor, agent or employee, or (b) is party to an effective confidentiality agreement with the Recipient which is consistent with the terms of this Agreement; *and* (2) has a need to know the Confidential Information in connection with the Project.

2. REQUIRED CONFIDENTIALITY

2.1 The parties and the respective employees will treat the Confidential Information as strictly confidential and proprietary, and will safeguard its confidential and proprietary nature with at least the same degree of care as they hold their own confidential or proprietary information.

2.2 Recipient may use the Confidential Information only in connection with the Project, and for no other purpose whatsoever. Recipient will not use the Confidential Information for the personal benefit of itself or a Permitted User, or for the benefit of any third party.

2.3 Recipient will not disclose (directly or indirectly) any Confidential Information to, or permit it to be accessed by, any person except a Permitted User. Recipient will cause any Permitted User to whom Confidential Information is disclosed to abide by the confidentiality provisions of this Agreement. On a case-by-case basis, either party may waive the restrictions of this Section 2.3 to provide for specific disclosures to specific third parties; provided, however, that such waiver must be in writing signed by the Disclosing Party and such third party must execute a confidentiality agreement with the Disclosing Party, which is consistent with the terms of this Agreement.

2.4 If Recipient is requested to disclose the Confidential Information or the substance of this Agreement in connection with a legal or administrative proceeding or otherwise to comply with a requirement under the law, Recipient will give the Disclosing Party prompt notice of such request so that the Disclosing Party may seek an appropriate protective order or other remedy, or waive compliance with the relevant provisions of this Agreement. If the Disclosing Party seeks a protective order or other remedy, Recipient, at Disclosing Party's expense, will cooperate with and assist the Disclosing Party in such efforts. If the Disclosing Party fails to obtain a protective order or waives compliance with the relevant provisions of this Agreement, Recipient will disclose only that portion of Confidential Information which its legal counsel determines it is required to disclose.

2.5 At the end of the Disclosure Period or upon completion of the Project, whichever is earlier, each party will use best efforts to promptly return all Confidential Information of the other party (including all copies in whatever medium provided to, or made by, any Permitted User).

2.6 Recipient agrees that it shall not modify, reverse engineer, decompile, create other works from or disassemble any Confidential Information unless permitted in writing by the Disclosing Party.

3 GENERAL PROVISIONS

3.1 All obligations of confidentiality will terminate after three (3) years from the termination date of the confidentiality agreement.

3.2 The parties represent and warrant to each other that each has the legal power and authority to enter into this Agreement and to disclose the Confidential Information.

3.3 Neither this Agreement, nor either party's performance under it, will (a) transfer to the Recipient, or create in the Recipient, any proprietary right, title, interest or claim in or to any of the Disclosing Party's Confidential Information; (b) obligate either party to enter into any other agreement or undertaking of any nature whatsoever with the other party; (c) prohibit either party from entering into any other agreement with any other party, if doing so will not violate such party's obligations hereunder; or (d) be construed as granting a license to the Confidential Information to either party.

3.4 This Agreement sets forth the entire understanding between the parties as to the subject matter, and supersedes all prior agreements and understandings relating to such subject matter.

3.5 This Agreement shall be governed by, and construed and enforced in accordance with the laws of <COUNTRY>, excluding its conflict of law rules.

3.6 The parties acknowledge that except as expressly set forth herein, (a) neither party has made any promise to the other, express or implied, upon which either is entitled to rely in any way; and (b) the parties specifically waive and disclaim any reliance, dependence or action based on any written or verbal statement or promise made by either party to the other.

3.7 Neither the rights nor the obligations of either party may be assigned or delegated, in whole or in part, without the prior written consent of the other party. Any such assignment or delegation shall be null and void and of no effect.

3.8 This Agreement may be executed by facsimile and/or in one or more counterparts, each of which shall be deemed an original, but all of which together shall constitute one and the same instrument.

3.9 If any term of this Agreement or the application thereof shall be deemed invalid or unenforceable, the remainder of this Agreement shall be unaffected thereby and each remaining term of this Agreement shall be valid and enforced to the fullest extent permitted by law.

3.10 A separate project-specific non-disclosure and business agreement will be put in place by both parties as needed.

The failure of either party to insist upon the strict observation or performance of any provision of this Agreement or to exercise any right or remedy shall not impair or waive any such right or remedy in the future. Every right and remedy given by this Agreement to the parties may be exercised from time to time as often as appropriate.

IN WITNESS WHEREOF the parties hereto have caused their duly authorized representatives to set their hands hereunder the <date>.

Signatures

<Name> — Date

<Title>

<COMPANY NAME>

Witness 1: <Name> — Date

<Name> — Date

<Title>

<COMPANY NAME>

Witness 2: <Name> — Date

Source: Based on Ghent University, Belgium, template.

Appendix 2
An example of an MTA

MATERIAL TRANSFER AGREEMENT

This Agreement is made on this <DAY>, <MONTH>, <YEAR> ("Effective Date") between

<COMPANY NAME A>

Address

(Hereinafter referred to as "<Company Name A>")

And

<COMPANY NAME B>

Address

(Hereinafter referred to as "<Company Name B>")

Hereinafter individually referred to as the "Party" and collectively as the "Parties"

WHEREAS, <Company Name> is engaged in the business etc.

WHEREAS, <Company Name> is engaged in the business etc.

WHEREAS, the parties are in the process of discussing potential etc.

WHEREAS, the parties acknowledge that their discussions might lead to some form etc.

WHEREAS, the parties desire to protect the confidentiality of certain information either may disclose to the other party through this agreement.

THEREFORE, in consideration of mutual promises and other valuable information exchanged and intended to be legally binding, the parties hereby agree and contract as follows.

1. DEFINITIONS

1.1 "Affiliates" means with respect to each party, the legal entities that control, are controlled by, or are under common control with such party.

1.2 "Confidential Information" shall be deemed to include information on <SUBJECT> and includes (a) the following types of information, whether or not so declared in writing: discoveries, techniques, know-how, ideas, concepts, formulations, molecules, structures, drug delivery regimes, designs, drawings, specifications, techniques, models, prototypes, data, source code, object code, documentation, manuals, diagrams, flow charts, schematics, research, process, procedures, functions, and all analyses, compilations, forecasts, studies or other documents, marketing techniques and materials, marketing and development plans, customer names and other information related to customer price lists, pricing policies and financial information, any and all related materials, inventions, practices, methods, knowledge, skill experience, test data, analytical and quality control data and manufacturing and patent data or descriptions; (b) any similar information disclosed to the Receiving Party or its employees prior to the execution of this Agreement; (c) any material transfer from the Disclosing Party to the Receiving Party along with the relevant proprietary information.

The term "Confidential Information" shall include any and all information and other materials disclosed, furnished, communicated, perceived or supplied by one party to the other party or by virtue of the one party visiting, witnessing and/or observing the facilities, laboratories or factory of the other party and/or its affiliate companies or associates could be reasonably assumed to be Confidential Information. Any information disclosed on <SUBJECT> by one party will be considered Confidential Information of the party by the other party whether or not such information is designated as "Confidential" or "Proprietary", or identified during the course of an oral disclosure as confidential.

1.3 "Disclosing Party" means the party or its employees that disclose Confidential Information to the other party (Recipient).

1.4 Disclosure Period" means the period during which either party may be disclosing Confidential Information to the other party. The Disclosure Period shall commence from the effective date set forth above, and shall expire <NUMBER> year(s) after such date, unless terminated earlier in writing by mutual agreement of the parties or upon the request of either party in writing.

1.5 "Recipient" means the party or its employees who receive Confidential Information from the other party (Disclosing Party).

1.6 "Exempt Information" means information that the Recipient can demonstrate by written records (a) was in its possession prior to the time of disclosure; (b) is or becomes public knowledge through no fault, omission, or other act of the Receiving Party; (c) is obtained from a third party under no obligation of confidentiality to the Disclosing Party; or (d) was independently developed by or for the Recipient without violating the terms of this Agreement.

1.7 "Permitted User" means an individual who (1) (a) is the Recipient's director, officer, consultant, financial advisor, agent or employee, or (b) is party to an effective confidentiality agreement with the Recipient which is consistent with the terms of this Agreement; and (2) has a need to know the Confidential Information in connection with the Project.

1.8 "Material" shall mean original material, unmodified derivatives, modifications, other derivatives, and their progeny.

1.9 "Progeny" shall mean unmodified descendants, including but not limited to virus from virus, cell from cell, vector from vector, or organism from organism.

1.10 The following aspects and related information of the material are considered to be confidential by the provider: identity, structure, sequence, characteristics, conformation, origin of the material, and the uses to which it is or may be put.

1.11 "Unmodified derivatives" shall mean substances created by the recipient which constitute an unmodified functional sub-unit or product expressed by the original material.

1.12 "Other derivatives" shall mean any and all material and/or substances, other than unmodified derivatives, modifications that are made, developed and/or otherwise created by the Recipient through the use of the original material, unmodified derivatives or modifications.

1.13 "Modifications" shall mean substances created by the Recipient which contain/incorporate the material.

1.14 "Commercial purposes": the sale, lease, license, or other transfer of the material or modifications to a for-profit organization.

Commercial purposes shall also include uses of the material or modifications by any organization, including the Recipient, to perform contract research, to screen compound libraries, to produce or manufacture products for general sale, or to conduct research activities that result in any sale, lease, license, or transfer of the material or modifications to a for-profit organization. However, industrially sponsored academic research shall not be considered a use of the material or modifications for commercial purposes *per se*, unless any of the above conditions of this definition are met.

THEREFORE, the Parties agree and contract as follows.

1. OWNERSHIP AND USE OF MATERIAL

1.1 Materials will include, but not be limited to, all formulae and all material embodied in the Materials, including derivatives and modifications to the Materials and related information.

1.2 <COMPANY B> will supply Materials to <COMPANY A> as specified in Attachment 1. <COMPANY A> agrees to return to <COMPANY B> all Materials not utilized before the Project Completion Date.

1.3 <COMPANY B> retains all rights, title and interest in the Materials.

1.4 No commercial license from <COMPANY B> is given or implied by the transfer of the Materials to <COMPANY A> or by this Agreement.

1.5 Materials will not be further distributed by <COMPANY A> to any third party without <COMPANY B's> written permission, nor used for commercial purposes.

1.6 Materials will be used for the Project only and specifically for evaluating the effectiveness of the Materials as <PURPOSE> at <COMPANY A>.

1.7 <COMPANY A> shall provide to <COMPANY B> a final report no later than thirty (30) days after the Project Completion Date of <DATE>.

1.8 The Parties each acknowledge that the Materials are proprietary. The Parties recognize the possibility of reverse engineering of the Materials through physical and chemical analysis and that such reverse engineering will seriously compromise <COMPANY B's> commercial position. Therefore, <COMPANY A> agrees not to reverse engineer the Materials.

2. REQUIRED CONFIDENTIALITY

2.1 The Materials and related subject matter are Confidential Information. <COMPANY A> will exercise due care to prevent unauthorized disclosure of Confidential Information except for subject matter and information.

2.2 Recipient may use the Confidential Information only in connection with the Project, and for no other purpose whatsoever. Recipient will not use the Confidential Information for the personal benefit of itself or a Permitted User, or for the benefit of any third party.

2.3. Recipient will not disclose (directly or indirectly) any Confidential Information to, or permit it to be accessed by, any person except a Permitted User. Recipient will cause any Permitted User to whom Confidential Information is disclosed to abide by the confidentiality provisions of this Agreement. On a case-by-case basis, either party may waive the restrictions of this Section 2.3 to provide for specific disclosures to specific third parties; provided, however, that such waiver must be in writing signed by the Disclosing Party and such third party must execute a confidentiality agreement with the Disclosing Party which is consistent with the terms of this Agreement.

2.4 If Recipient is requested to disclose the Confidential Information or the substance of this Agreement in connection with a legal or administrative proceeding or otherwise to comply with a requirement under the law, Recipient will give the Disclosing Party prompt notice of such request so that the Disclosing Party may seek an appropriate protective order or other remedy, or waive compliance with the relevant provisions of this Agreement. If the Disclosing Party seeks a protective order or other remedy, Recipient, at Disclosing Party's expense, will cooperate with and assist Disclosing Party in such efforts. If the Disclosing Party fails to obtain a protective order or waives compliance with the relevant provisions of this Agreement, Recipient will disclose only that portion of Confidential Information which its legal counsel determines it is required to disclose.

2.5 At the end of the Disclosure Period or upon completion of the Project, whichever is earlier, each party will use best efforts to promptly return all Confidential Information of the other party (including all copies in whatever medium provided to, or made by, any Permitted User).

2.6 Recipient agrees that it shall not modify, reverse engineer, de-compile, create other works from or disassemble any Confidential Information unless permitted in writing by the Disclosing Party.

3. GENERAL PROVISIONS

3.1 All obligations of confidentiality will terminate after three (3) years from the termination date of the confidentiality agreement.

3.2 The parties represent and warrant to each other that each has the legal power and authority to enter into this Agreement and to disclose the Confidential Information.

3.3 Neither this Agreement, nor either party's performance under it, will (a) transfer to the Recipient, or create in the Recipient, any proprietary right, title, interest or claim in or to any of the Disclosing Party's Confidential Information; (b) obligate either party to enter into any other agreement or undertaking of any nature whatsoever with the other party; (c) prohibit either party from entering into any other agreement with any other party, if doing so will not violate such party's obligations hereunder; or (d) be construed as granting a license to the Confidential Information to either party.

3.4 This Agreement sets forth the entire understanding between the parties as to the subject matter, and supersedes all prior agreements and understandings relating to such subject matter.

3.5 This Agreement shall be governed by, and construed and enforced in accordance with the laws of <COUNTRY>, excluding its conflict of law rules.

3.6 The parties acknowledge that except as expressly set forth herein, (a) neither party has made any promise to the other, express or implied, upon which either is entitled to rely in any way; and (b) the parties specifically waive and disclaim any reliance, dependence or action based on any written or verbal statement or promise made by either party to the other.

3.7 Neither the rights nor the obligations of either party may be assigned or delegated, in whole or in part, without the prior written consent of the other party. Any such assignment or delegation shall be null and void and of no effect.

3.8 This Agreement may be executed by facsimile and/or in one or more counterparts, each of which shall be deemed an original, but all of which together shall constitute one and the same instrument.

3.9 If any term of this Agreement or the application thereof shall be deemed invalid or unenforceable, the remainder of this Agreement shall be unaffected thereby and each remaining term of this Agreement shall be valid and enforced to the fullest extent permitted by law.

3.10 A separate project-specific non-disclosure and business agreement will be put in place by both parties as needed.

The failure of either party to insist upon the strict observation or performance of any provision of this Agreement, or to exercise any right or remedy, shall not impair or waive any such right or remedy in the future. Every right and remedy given by this Agreement to the parties may be exercised from time to time as often as appropriate.

IN WITNESS WHEREOF the parties hereto have caused their duly authorized representatives to set their hands hereunder the <DATE>.

Signatures

______________________	______________________
<Name> <Title> <COMPANY NAME>	Date
______________________	______________________
Witness 1: <Name>	Date
______________________	______________________
<Name> <Title> <COMPANY NAME>	Date
______________________	______________________
Witness 2: <Name>	Date

Attachment 1

Description of the materials
(Give description, sample size, safety aspects, etc.)

Materials will be shipped to:
Contact name:

Title:

Company name:

Street address:

City:

Country:

Zip:

Phone:

Facsimile:

Email:

Source: Based on Ghent University, Belgium, template.

Appendix 3
Invention disclosure form

Purpose

Completing this document is the first step towards protecting and commercializing your invention.

The purpose of the invention disclosure form (IDF) is to provide a written, dated record of your invention from which your technology can be evaluated. It enables the technology transfer (TT) office of your institution to determine if the technology is patentable and identify possible opportunities for commercializing it.

When to submit

An IDF should be completed when something new and useful has been conceived or developed or when unusual, unexpected, or unobvious research results have been achieved and can be utilized. It is important that the disclosure is made as early and as completely as possible, although it may be amended at a later stage.

All commercially valuable research results have to be reported before any form of public disclosure.

To prevent loss of patent rights, we strongly recommend contacting your institution before submitting any invention-related manuscripts for publication, making oral presentations, or disclosing the invention to companies or other third parties.

Inventors

Correctly identifying all individuals who contributed to the technology is very important. Inventorship is not the same as authorship and has important legal implications.

Format

The document is written in English to facilitate screening by an outside counsel if needed.

Do not modify the form. If questions do not apply, indicate NA. Add spaces and table rows as needed. Please email the completed and fully signed document. The original copy is also required.

Where to submit

Return the completed and signed disclosure document along with supporting documentation to the following address: (provide address)

Further information

For advice on completing the disclosure document or additional information, do not hesitate to contact your institution.

Date: Location:

1. Title of the invention (+ possible acronym).
2. Related business area.
3. Description of the invention.
   - If you would consider your invention as a solution, what technical problem were you trying to solve (if multiple problems, please identify each)?
   - How have others tried to solve this problem? Describe for each solution the functional and/or structural differences with your solution.

- Describe the advantage(s) of your solution over the existing solutions.
- Give a short description of the invention, preferably including a list of those elements of the invention that are essential to make it work, those elements that can be varied, and how they can be varied (max. one page).
- Does your invention possess disadvantages or limitations? Indicate how they might be overcome.
- Describe the development status (concept only, laboratory tested, *in vitro*/*in vivo* data, prototype, etc.). Indicate what further development may be necessary.

4. Invention disclosure record.
   List all past and near-future *disclosures of the invention* (or parts of it). If unpublished and undisclosed, provide the anticipated disclosure date and any submissions already made for potential publication.

Type	Title, Date and Reference:
Licensor	Title: Date: Reference:
Oral presentation(s) at meetings, conferences, companies...	Title: Date: Reference:
Abstract, poster, or proceeding has been or will be posted, printed, or web-published (faculty and other websites).	Title: Date: Reference:
A manuscript(s) describing the invention has been or will be submitted for publication (also internet pre-publishing!).	Title: Date: Reference:

A manuscript describing the invention has been or will be published.	Title: Date: Reference:
A thesis (undergraduate, master or doctoral) describing the invention has been or will be submitted and defended. * Be aware: also consider summaries, invitations to public defense, and submissions to the library. Please check with the TT adviser before disclosure.	Title: Date: Reference:
A report (official or internal) that describes the invention.	Title: Date: Reference:
A news article or feature report describing the invention has been or will be printed or published on the web.	Title: Date: Reference:
Information describing the invention has been or will be given to a person, company, or institution outside the present institution with a confidentiality agreement (CDA/NDA). Please provide contract number and date.	Title: Date: Reference:
Information describing the invention has been or will be given (date) to a person, company, or institution outside the present institution without a confidentiality agreement (CDA/NDA).	Title: Date: Reference:

5. Prior art.
   - Please list and attach copies of *any publication made by the inventors* believed by you to disclose ideas *most closely related* to the invention.
   - Please list and attach copies of *any publication of others* (theses, reports, preprints, reprints, papers, abstracts, or internet publications) believed by you to disclose ideas *most closely related* to the invention.
   - Is literature screened on a regular basis?

     Yes ☐ No ☐

     If yes, please provide keywords:
   - Please list *any patent or patent application of others* believed by you to disclose ideas *most closely related* to the invention. A publicly available patent database is e.g. http://be.espacenet.com or http://www.wipo.org.
   - Who are the main academic or industrial research groups *active in the field* (e.g. name/organization)?

6. Inventors.

Name only those who contributed *intellectually* to the inventive concept of the invention.

> Note: Inventorship is not the same as authorship and has important legal implications!
> An inventor is one who makes an intellectual contribution to the inventive idea or concept. A person who merely carries out the ideas and suggestions of others or simply provides support (materials, financial means) is not an inventor.
> If you are not certain, please contact your institution.

Inventor 1 – contact person for your institution

Said inventor is responsible for:

- providing scientific input to the institution
- providing requested documents to the institution and the patent agent assigned to the invention
- communicating with co-inventors, institution, and patent agent
- notifying the institution of changes in the development status of the invention.

Name:

Institution/dept.:

Address (work):

Email:

Phone:

Address (home):

Citizenship:

Contribution to the invention (indicate what + %):

Institution's payroll: Yes ☐ No ☐

And/or others:

Inventor 2

Name:

Institution/dept.:

Address (work):

Email:

Phone:

Address (home):

Citizenship:

Contribution to the invention (indicate what + %):

Institution's payroll: Yes ☐ No ☐

Inventor 3

Name:

Institution/dept.:

Address (work):

Email:

Phone:

Address (home):

Citizenship:

Contribution to the invention (indicate what + %):

Institution's payroll: Yes ☐ No ☐

(Add additional names if required.)

7. Records/material.
   - Are lab records available? Are these lab records dated and signed?
   - At what site(s) was the research conducted that led to the invention?
   - Does the invention incorporate any material obtained from companies or institutions outside the institution? If so, has a material transfer agreement (MTA) been signed for this material? Please give the contract number and list material, date received, and supplier.
8. Funding.
   - Past and current funding that led to the invention.

Agency or sponsor	Grant/contract type and reference number	Term (dd/mm/yy to dd/mm/yy)

   - Future funding that will further develop/improve the invention. If work on the invention is to be continued, indicate known or probable sources of funding and the nature of the work yet to be performed.
9. Collaboration.
   - Is the invention the result of a collaborative project involving another party?
   - Is there a contract/agreement? If yes, please provide contract number.
10. Authorship/copyright.
   - Is there any expression of this invention through software?
   - What is the purpose of the software (e.g. proof of concept, demonstration of invention, prototype, fully functional end-user version)?
   - Is the software a derivative or improvement of any existing source code? If so, which?
11. Commercialization potential.
   - In your opinion, what kind of commercial applications could be derived from your invention and how easy/feasible would it be to

bring a product to the market (e.g. high development/regulatory burden, need for third-party technologies)?
- Which companies or customers could be interested in your invention?

12. Signatures.

Signing this document indicates that:

- the IDF is complete and accurate
- the inventors recognize that commercialization of their invention will require a commitment of their time towards technology assessment, patenting, and commercialization processes.

Signatures of inventors (*Note:* All inventors must sign here)		
Name:	Signature:	Date:
Name:	Signature:	Date:
Name:	Signature:	Date:
(Add additional names if required.)		

Source: Based on Ghent University, Belgium, template.

Index

FSC
www.fsc.org
MIX
Papier | Fördert gute Waldnutzung
FSC® C083411

Kolibri 360 GmbH
Ferdinand-Jühlke-Straße 7
99095 Erfurt, Deutschland
produktsicherheit@kolibri360.de